VOLUNTEER VACATIONS

A Directory of Short-Term Adventures That Will Benefit You . . . And Others

Third Edition, Revised & Expanded

Bill McMillon

CHICAGO REVIEW PRESS

Library of Congress Catologing-in-Publication Data

McMillon, Bill, 1942–

Volunteer vacations : a directory of short-term adventures
    that will benefit you—and others / Bill McMillon.—Rev.
    and expanded ed., 3rd ed.
            p.   cm.
    Bibliography: p. 382
    Includes indexes.
    1. Voluntarism.   2. Associations, institutions, etc.—
directories.   3. Vacations.   I. Title.

Grateful acknowledgment is given to William Morrow &
Company for permission to reprint the quotation on page v:
excerpt from page 85 of *Aspects of the Present* by Magaret
Mead and Rhoda Metraux. Copyright ©1980 by Catherine
Bateson Kassarjian and Rhoda Metraux. Reprinted by per-
mission of William Morrow & Company, Inc.

Published by Chicago Review Press, Incorporated
814 N. Franklin Street, Chicago Illinois 60610
ISBN 1-55652-134-0
Printed in the United States of America
1 2 3 4 5 6 7 8 9 10

To Matt, who at age 16 disdainfully dropped an Earthwatch bulletin in my lap saying, "Here's something from another one of those weird programs." May you someday enjoy a vacation through one of those "weird" programs.

Contents

Foreword

It's been said that "man would rather spend himself for a cause than live idly in prosperity." I'm sure upon uttering that axiom in a group, you'd see everyone nodding wisely—agreeing that hard work for a cause is preferable to the good life unfulfilled. It's a noble thought during a philosophical discussion. When everyone's in accord on that point, pull out some airline tickets to Perryville, Arkansas, and ask who's willing to give up their Bermuda vacation in order to work with livestock. Any takers?

It's a hard sell. Public service is an antiquity in today's society. In the 1930s the CCC (Civilian Conservation Corps) instilled in the minds of young men and women the notion that national service is an obligation—indeed, a privilege: putting something back into the country in exchange for all the benefits derived from living in a free and democratic country. It was a wonderful setup and one that should have been perpetuated.

Since that time, however, our country's military bent has made national service anathema—national service has come to mean the draft, the military, risk of life and limb on some foreign shore. Some states, to supplement low budget allocations, use public service as punishment for misdemeanors: in Oregon, for instance, DWI offenders can be seen picking up highway litter.

In short, the notion of a "volunteer vacation" sounds like a disciplinary measure—something akin to assigning extra household chores to a balky teenager.

Happily, there are people like Bill McMillon (along with the hundreds of people who've taken volunteer vacations) to set us straight; volunteering for a worthy cause can be fun, fulfilling, and an adventure you'll anticipate year after year. Maybe working with livestock isn't your thing, but there's plenty of variety: go on archaeological expeditions . . . assist health care in remote villages . . . maintain trails in beautiful mountain climes . . . build homes for the homeless. Some programs encourage you to bring the kids; some pay for part of your expenses.

Best of all, you'll be helping people who need you. These days our local, state, and federal government budgets (and many government budgets around the world) have cut "people programs" in favor of big business and the military. More and more, our nation and our world must look to volunteers to full the gaps that governments are unwilling or unable to fill—in health care, education, programs for the handicapped and underprivileged.

Read this book . . . try a volunteer vacation. The world will be a better place—and so will you.

Edward Asner

Preface to the Third Edition

In the years since I began work on the first edition of *Volunteer Vacations*, public awareness of the possibilities of using their vacation time to help others has spread dramatically. Seldom does a week pass that I don't receive a copy of some newspaper or magazine article telling of an individual or group that has helped a needy organization by volunteering during the time most Americans use to escape from the real world into that nebulous idea called a vacation.

Ron Post uses his time off from his Salem, Oregon building firm to organize volunteer medical teams who spend two weeks in Third World countries. What began as a one-time project is now a full-time organization, Northwest Medical Teams.

Ron is often asked why he isn't spending his energy helping the needy in this country, and his response is, "I can say I am when I send people to the dumps of Mexico City or the Indian villages of Oaxaca and they see poverty that they have never seen in their lives. When they come back to this country, they are much more aware of the poverty around them."

Ron is obviously in touch with many segments of our population, for organizations such as his are very popular in the U.S., but so are the ones that work closer to home.

When an earthquake hit the San Francisco Bay area in October 1989, organizations such as Mennonite Disaster Services and the Christian Reformed World Relief Committee rushed in to help those who were unable to receive help from state and federal relief offices, just as they did in South Carolina to help survivors of Hurricane Hugo.

These efforts are not short-term; the organizations will stay in disaster areas as long as there is a need. Individuals come from near and far to work for varying periods of time, mostly short- term.

And not all of the volunteers are from the U.S. Many of

those who worked on the Mennonite Disaster Services project in San Francisco came from Canada, and a 1989 project in Yakima, Washington involved volunteers from even farther away. U.S. construction crews went to Soviet Armenia to help them rebuild after a devastating earthquake, and a group of ten Soviet citizens helped return the favor by spending six weeks in Yakima building four homes and a day-care center for poor farm workers.

Social action projects aren't the only ones profiting from this increase in the public's interest in volunteering. In 1989 the National Park Service Volunteers in the Parks program reported that over 54,000 people donated about $23 million worth of time performing a wide variety of jobs. On a smaller scale, more than 5,000 people participated on 110 Trail Days projects in California during two days in April 1990.

As you can see, you will be joining a large number of other people in the pursuit of happiness through giving during your vacation as you use this guide to help you find the right organization for you—the organization that will best allow you to use your vacation time to accomplish something positive, while actually re-creating how you approach your everyday life.

Betty Meyskens, who is featured in the vignette "Ms. America Goes to Nicaragua," has discovered that her life hasn't been the same since her volunteer effort. She has maintained contact with the village she worked in, organized a women's church group that regularly contacts a similar group in Nicaragua, and is returning to the village in the spring of 1991 for a second volunteer project.

Not all people who volunteer end up with their lives dramatically changed, but few ever forget their first volunteer vacation.

Acknowledgments

Obviously, a guide such as this could never have been compiled without the cooperation and assistance of the hundreds of organizations that accept short-term volunteers, and I deeply appreciate their willingness to share their needs with me. I would especially like to thank all the people behind the scenes at these organizations who took time out from their heavy schedules to answer my questions, and supply me with vignettes and photos. I would also like to thank Linda, who saw the potential and bought my proposal; Amy, who pushed hard for more and better in the first two editions of; and Julie, who made sure that word about *Volunteer Vacations* was spread far and wide.

We live in a society that always has depended on volunteers of different kinds—some who can give money, others who give time and a great many who will freely give their special skills, full-time or part-time. If you look closely you will see that almost anything that really matters to us, anything that embodies our deepest commitment to the way human life should be lived and cared for depends on some form—more often many forms—of volunteerism.

Margaret Mead and Rhoda Metraux
Aspects of the Present

Introduction

"What's a volunteer vacation?"
"One where you work for some organization on a special project."
"You mean really work? On your vacation?"
"Right."
"Who would want to do that?"

This imaginary conversation is often quoted as I promote this guide on radio and TV programs. Many interviewers really can't grasp the idea that tens of thousands of people take volunteer vacations each year.

Obviously, some people can't envision working on a vacation. Others, however, find doing so a refreshing change of pace.

If you are one of the latter, or think you might be, and want to work on something other than projects around the house during your next vacation, this book can be a passport to vacation happiness. Nineteen-year-old Rory Camp used this passport when he volunteered for a summer at the Theodore Roosevelt National Park in North Dakota with the Student Conservation Association. Nobel and Frances Dubach, in their early seventies, have used it for over 10 years as volunteer hosts at the U.S. Forest Service campground at Brainard Lake in the Roosevelt National Park in Colorado.

More and more people are finding this happiness by volunteering to work for organizations that need help completing scientific, ecological, social service, and other projects that can't be handled by regular staff because of personnel or financial problems. These projects can be near home or in a foreign land. Distance matters less than the deep satisfaction that can be gained from doing worthwhile work of a type you normally don't have an opportunity to do.

1

HOW TO SELECT A VOLUNTEER PROJECT

There is no shortage of volunteer projects. Some are near home; others are across the oceans. Some are helping to complete scientific investigations; others lead to social change. Some cost nothing but your travel expenses to the project site; others are more expensive than traditional guided tours.

The one you select will depend upon your needs and abilities—physical, emotional, intellectual, and financial.

WHAT THIS GUIDE TELLS YOU

This guide is divided into two sections. The first is an alphabetical listing of organizations that offer opportunities for volunteers: the types of projects offered, their locations, costs, dates, and requirements for volunteers. Interspersed throughout Part One are "Volunteer Vignettes," personal stories from travelers, both in the U.S. and abroad, who have taken a wide variety of volunteer vacations, and from those who have used short-term volunteers on a variety of projects.

Cross-Referenced Indexes

The second section provides cross-referenced indexes. Their purpose is to help you define the types of projects you are interested in and then to help you locate the organizations that offer such projects.

The indexes include: Project Cost (under $500, $500 to $999, $1,000 to $1,999, $2,000 and over); Project Length (under one week, one to two weeks, two to four weeks, and four to six weeks); Project Location (U.S., Europe, other areas of world); Project Season (winter, spring, summer, or fall); and Project Type (scientific, ecological, social action, and other special interests). Each index lists organizations that offer one or more projects that meet the criteria for that index.

To use the indexes, begin by defining your criteria for a volunteer vacation. The first step probably will be deciding what subject area interests you. This could be anything from digging fossils to helping in a soup kitchen. You can then decide where you would like to pursue this subject, how much you want to spend on your trip, what time of year you

2

want to go, and how long you want to be gone.

Let's say you want to work on an archaeological dig in the U.S. for two weeks during the summer, and keep costs other than travel to the project site to less than $500. You would first look in the Project Type Index to find a list of organizations that have archaeological excavation projects. You can then compare this list against the Location Index to come up with a shorter list of organizations that offer digs in the U.S.

Then compare this list against the project season, cost, and length indexes in turn to come up with your final list, which will give you a list of organizations that offer two-week archaeological dig projects, during the summer, in the U.S., for under $500.

You can now return to the first section of the book and read about the organizations on your list; then you can contact those that seem to fit your needs and find out if they have vacancies on the projects that interest you.

GENERAL INFORMATION

Although each project differs, there are some general characteristics that you can expect most of them to have.

Transportation Almost all projects require volunteers to arrange and pay for their own transportation to the project site. The exception is the final leg to isolated sites; the sponsoring organization generally arranges this portion of the trip.

Special Requirements and Skills Although some projects have no requirements for volunteers other than an interest and a willingness to work, others have very specific requirements. Many of the Sierra Club and American Hiking Society projects, for example, require superb physical conditioning. Other expeditions may require special skills such as scuba certification.

No project allows unqualified volunteers to register, however, so there are no on-site surprises for volunteers or project leaders.

Food and Housing Many of the projects arrange for housing for all volunteers, along with some provision for meals.

3

Both food and housing range from the bare minimum to semi-luxurious, and this is generally stated in the project brochure. On other projects volunteers are responsible for their own food and housing.

What to Bring Again, each project is different, and each requires different types of clothing, equipment, and house-keeping gear. After you have been accepted for a project, you will receive a list of articles that are recommended for your comfort and for working on the project. Follow this list closely, and contact your project leader if you have any questions. Not only your comfort, but the comfort of the other volunteers may be involved.

Most volunteers like to bring a camera to record their trip, but, again, the project leader should be contacted to see what special precautions should be taken with photographic equipment, since many of the projects are in isolated locations where climatic conditions can cause serious problems for cameras and lenses.

Group Interactions These projects are done in groups, and while some are larger than others, volunteers on any project must be prepared to spend extended time in close contact with a group of strangers. This means dealing with unpleasant situations as well as enjoyable ones. While the project leaders interviewed for this guide emphasized that most projects have few problems within the groups, they said there were occasional conflicts that just had to be worked out on the site.

Tax Information The media has emphasized the tax advantages of volunteer vacations, but not everyone qualifies for them. To deduct your expenses for a volunteer vacation, there are several conditions that must be met. The most important one is that the organization must be registered with the Internal Revenue Service as a tax-exempt, nonprofit corporation; and many of the organizations in this guide are. But there are exceptions, such as the Sierra Club and foreign organizations.

The only way to ensure a tax write-off is to contact a knowledgeable tax accountant before registering for a trip.

WHAT THIS GUIDE DOESN'T TELL YOU

It is difficult, if not impossible, for any guide that covers as broad a range of activities as this one does, to comprehensively evaluate the organizations and how they run their projects. All of the organizations included here are reputable, and they have served thousands of volunteers over the years, but it would be impossible for all of those volunteers to have had only positive experiences. There are just too many variables.

The only way you can find out if a particular organization is one that you will feel comfortable with is to contact them directly, ask specific and pointed questions of the staff, and locate some previous volunteers to interview.

Even with these precautions there are no guarantees, but that is one of the positive aspects of volunteer vacations. People who want guarantees go on guided tours. Those who want adventure and a change of pace go on volunteer vacations.

Participants in Intersea Research expeditions often get this view of humpback whales. (Photo courtesy of Cynthia D'Vincent)

Opportunities for volunteers are so numerous that it would be impossible to mention them all. If you are interested in finding out more about volunteering, look around your hometown. Ask about subjects you are interested in, and see if any of your acquaintances have ever volunteered for some related project. Contact a state or national organization that is concerned and involved with your area of interest to see if they know of any local volunteer possibilities.

More and more large companies are helping employees find volunteers positions in their communities. Wells Fargo, one of the largest banks in California, has an extensive program that encourages employees to volunteer in their hometown, and even offers sabbaticals so volunteers can spend extended periods of time on projects. Xerox and IBM have similar programs.

These companies also regularly publish volunteer bulletins for employees listing volunteer opportunities.

The State of California has brought volunteerism to the campuses of its two major university systems. In 1988 the state legislature passed AB 1820, the "Human Corps" bill, and Governor George Deukmejian signed it into law. With that law California legislated a policy stating that all students enrolled at the 29 campuses of the California State University system and the 9 campuses of the University of California are expected to provide at least 30 hours of community service each year, and each campus is developing a list of volunteer opportunities for its students.

And the hundreds of volunteer centers around the country often publish a list of current needs in the Help Wanted sections of their local papers.

Together, all of these demonstrate the heavy role that volunteering plays in our society.

If you are interested in volunteering and already know what opportunities are available locally, but want to find out more about what's going on nationally and internationally, this guide can help you get started.

Each of the organizations listed handles the recruitment of volunteers differently. Some do all of their own recruiting, while others use one of several organizations that have sprung up in the past two decades to match potential volunteers with projects needing help.

One of the largest of these is Earthwatch; it has been described as the "Yuppie Peace Corps," but don't let that label mislead you. Earthwatch and the rest of the organizations in this guide are much more than glorified travel agencies for well-to-do young people. All of them do serious, beneficial work, and most accept volunteers of all ages.

While groups that specialize in ecological or scientific work—such as Earthwatch, the Sierra Club, and the Cousteau Society—have garnered the most media attention in the past several years, they are actually minorities in this guide.

Projects run by, or for, religious groups, social service agencies, and other small special interest groups abound both in the U.S. and abroad. In fact, there is some project for almost everyone who is interested in working on his or her vacation. All you have to do is find the one that suits your needs. And this directory will simplify that process. While no volunteer guide could ever claim to be complete, this one offers a wide range of volunteer opportunities for people who want a short-term (one to six weeks) commitment.

OTHER SOURCES OF INFORMATION

Other sources, listed at the end of the book, can help those who want to take longer volunteer vacations, or who prefer to go on adventure or learning vacations without work commitments. Also included are several periodicals that include information about volunteer, learning, and adventure vacations.

Organizations

Several of the organizations listed in this guide work extensively with state and national parks and with the U.S. Forest Service, and although some of their offices are also listed in the guide, there are always new projects that need volunteers but aren't listed anywhere. Many campgrounds offer free camping to their volunteer hosts, who assist other campers in return. Ministers often are given free camping privileges in exchange for performing services on Sunday. And some national forests offer free housing to people who are willing to be volunteer naturalists at isolated sites.

Contact either regional offices or national headquarters for these agencies to find out about unlisted volunteer opportunities.

Religious groups offer many volunteer opportunities for social activists, and colleges and universities often offer summer courses that serve as vehicles for gaining research assistants. Colleges and universities also offer many travel courses through their extension programs.

For those over 55, an interesting program is Elderhostel, which is held on college and university campuses, using regular faculty, throughout the year. To find out more about this program, contact Elderhostel, 100 Boylston St., Suite 200, Boston MA 02116.

Service organizations are another possible source of information.

Remember, volunteer opportunities are unlimited. It is just a matter of finding a project that suits you. After all, it is your vacation.

Volunteer Vacations Update

While it is possible in a guide such as this to include considerable information about the many organizations that are included, it just isn't feasible to include an exhaustive list of the projects currently being offered by any of them. The publishing process is just too long. Any project listing would be out-of-date long before the guide ever reached the bookstores.

Many readers mentioned this as they read the first edition of *Volunteer Vacations*, and to fill this need I began a quarterly newsletter. This newsletter, *Volunteer Vacations Update*, gives specific information about upcoming projects being offered by organizations in this guide and lists new organizations that I have located since this edition *Volunteer Vacations* went to press.

To obtain a complimentary copy of *Volunteer Vacations Update* and subscription information, write to Bill McMillon, *Volunteer Vacations Update*, 2120 Green Hill Rd., Sebastopol CA 95472; tel. (707) 829-9364.

American Friends Service Committee summer project participants join with residents of Congregacion de la Cruz, in the Mexican state of Guanajuato, to build roads and homes. (Photo courtesy of American Friends Service Committee)

Part One

SPONSORING ORGANIZATIONS & VOLUNTEER VIGNETTES

Alaska Division of Parks and Outdoor Recreation

PO Box 107001
Anchorage AK 99510-7001
Phone changes frequently with seasonal change in coordinator.

Project Locations: Parks located statewide.
Project Types: Park management and maintenance.
Project Costs: Volunteers are responsible for transportation to and from Alaska.
Project Dates: Varying periods of time from May to September.
How To Apply: Write to Volunteer Coordinator at the above address for application and information packet.
Work Done by Volunteers: Campground hosts, visitor information center staff, backcountry patrol, trail crew, naturalist, and ranger assistant.
Special Skills or Requirements: No special skills are required, but volunteers with an interest in Alaska, a strong outdoor background, and good communications skills are preferred.
Commentary: Alaska State Parks began its volunteer program in 1983, when severe budget cuts forced the division to seek creative economic strategies. Since then hundreds of people have generously donated their time and energies to the continued preservation and management of Alaska's state parks. Park volunteers do not replace paid staff members. They supplement the existing staff and provide programs to the public that would otherwise not be available.

American Friends Service Committee

1501 Cherry St.
Philadelphia PA 19102-1479
tel. (215) 241-7000

Project Locations: Primarily Mexico, but occasionally other Latin American countries.

Project Types: There is no set pattern to these projects. Past projects have included construction of schools, clinics, roads, and houses, as well as reforestation, gardening, and health programs.

Project Costs: Participants pay $700 to cover orientation, insurance, and food and lodging at the project site. Volunteers are also responsible for their own transportation to the project site.

Project Dates: Most projects run for six weeks from the end of June to mid-August.

How To Apply: Send a letter of interest to American Friends Service Committee, Summer Community Service in Latin America, at the above address.

Work Done by Volunteers: All volunteers share in both the labor on the project itself, and in the normal living activities such as cooking, cleaning, weekly marketing, etc. All actively participate in the normal life of the village where they are living.

Special Skills or Requirements: Applicants should be between 18 and 26 years old and speak good Spanish, since it is the project language at all times. Construction, gardening, arts & crafts, recreation, and previous group experience are all useful.

Commentary: AFSC is a Quaker organization, and this service project is done in conjunction with a Mexican service organization. Each summer 50 volunteers are chosen to work on projects in Mexico, and they are divided into teams of 2 leaders and 15 volunteers to work in different villages.

Half of the volunteers are from Latin America, and the other half are from the U.S.

14

American Hiking Society

AHS—Volunteer Vacations
PO Box 86
North Scituate MA 02060

Project Locations: AHS has projects from Alaska to Wyoming, plus the U.S. Virgin Islands.

Project Types: All projects are trail building, trail maintenance, and similar work for the National Park Service, National Forest Service, or state park systems, primarily in remote locations.

Project Costs: $30 registration fee upon acceptance. Volunteers must furnish all of their own camping gear and equipment, and all transportation to the project site. AHS arranges for the final leg of the trip to remote sites. Insurance is provided while participants are working. Cooperating agencies supply hard hats, tools, and food. AHS sometimes finds donors for food.

Project Dates: Projects are for two weeks and are generally held in June, July, and August, with an occasional project in May or September. Previous projects in Hawaii and U.S. Virgin Islands have been held in January.

How To Apply: Send a self-addressed, stamped long envelope for an application and list of projects to AHS—Volunteer Vacations at the above address. Apply as early as possible, for many of these projects fill quickly.

Work Done by Volunteers: Hard manual labor in rugged, remote locations, many at high altitudes.

Special Skills or Requirements: Must be an experienced backpacker who can easily hike 5 to 10 miles a day and live outdoors for a two-week stretch. Applicants under 18 must have their parents' permission, and those under 16 must be accompanied by an adult.

Commentary: The AHS—Volunteer Vacation program began in 1979 with 30 volunteers working at two Forest Service sites. It now has over 300 volunteers each year, with about one-third of the volunteers returning from previous years.

Since many of the sites are in very remote and rugged areas, volunteers can expect to explore some of the outstanding wilderness in the U.S., while sharing this experience with 10 to 12 other volunteers. Supervision at most of the sites is done by National Park or Forest Service personnel.

Sample Projects: Following are a few projects AHS volunteers have worked on:

Admiralty Island National Monument in Alaska—helping maintain three cabins on Hassleborg Lake. General maintenance and cutting firewood for each cabin.

Buffalo National River in Arkansas—continuing work on a new section of the Ozark Trail.

Haleakala National Park in Hawaii—working on exotic plant control in different areas of the park. Volunteers hiked approximately 10 miles each day as they uprooted or sprayed exotic plants.

American Mexican Medical Foundation (AMMEX)

Route 3, Box 123
Princeton MN 55371
tel. (612) 389-5164

Project Location: Durango, Mexico.
Project Types: Health and community development.
Project Costs: Volunteers are responsible for travel expenses and approximately $10 per day for food and miscellaneous expenses.
Project Dates: Vary, but typically August, December, and May.
How To Apply: Send a letter including information on your background and interests to the above address.
Work Done by Volunteers: Common activities screening and collecting data in a health clinic, distributing food and clothing, constructing or repairing homes, and becoming involved in various family assistance projects.
Special Skills or Requirements: Although no special skills are required, AMMEX prefers that volunteers have some Spanish, and always welcomes volunteers with special medical or construction skills.
Commentary: AMMEX was begun in 1969 as Roger and Eva Belisle began making Mercy trips into remote and isolated areas of Mexico. After a time they began taking friends with them as volunteers. From that came the idea for forming a nonprofit organization devoted to helping the residents of Durango. While interest in the project has grown over the years, the bulk of the work and funding that keeps AMMEX going still comes from the Belisles, and this very special organization is very much in need of continued and expanded support.

American Rivers

801 Pennsylvania Ave., SE, #303
Washington DC 20003
tel. (202) 547-6900

Project Location: Washington, DC.
Project Types: A variety of intern positions are available each year.
Project Costs: Participants are responsible for all living costs.
Project Dates: Throughout the year, although summer positions are the most popular.
How To Apply: Send resume and cover letter to Sheryl Schultz, Intern Coordinator, at the above address.
Work Done by Volunteers: Depends upon assignment.
Special Skills or Requirements: An intense interest in saving America's rivers, and in the environment in general.
Commentary: American Rivers is the nation's principal river-saving organization. It is the only nonprofit charitable group devoted exclusively to preserving the nation's outstanding rivers and their landscapes. It measures its success in river miles and streamside acres protected, unneeded dams blocked, and taxpayer dollars saved.
Sample Projects: Interns focus on a single project during their time in Washington, and every effort is made to match their interests with the needs of the organization.

Amigos de las Americas
5618 Star Lane
Houston TX 77057
tel. (800) 231- 7796; in Texas (713) 782-5290

Project Locations: Throughout Latin America.

Project Types: Wide variety of public health projects.

Project Costs: From $2,020 to $2,450, plus round-trip travel to Houston, Texas. This cost covers training materials, transportation from Houston to host country, and field supplies. Host country provides food and housing.

Project Dates: Projects are for four, six, or eight weeks and run from mid-June to mid-August.

How To Apply: Contact Amigos de las Americas at the above address for information on where local chapters are located, or for information about their correspondent training program for volunteers. There is a March 1 application deadline.

Work Done by Volunteers: Wide variety of public health projects, from helping plan and dig public latrines, to canoeing through tropical rain forests to inoculate against yellow fever, to distributing medical supplies in local settlements. All projects are done under the supervision of a route leader who lives in host country and is experienced with Amigos.

Special Skills or Requirements: Volunteers must speak at least minimal Spanish, be at least 16 years old, and have completed the Amigos training program. Although the majority of the volunteers are high school and college students, there is no upper age limit.

Commentary: Amigos began in 1965 as a religious organization, but has since dropped all association with any church or religion. It has maintained its benevolent spirit, however, and has placed over 10,000 volunteers in 13 Latin American countries in the past 20 years. Most of these have been youth who have been given responsibilities far beyond those normally accorded them in the U.S. Consequently they have returned home with an appreciation of others, and a sensitivity to them, that far surpasses their peers.

Sample Projects: Amigos has had projects in Mexico, Costa Rica, Ecuador, Paraguay, and the Dominican Republic that taught dental hygiene, developed community sanitation projects, gave immunizations, did vision screening, and provided animal health services.

Andover Foundation for Archaeological Research

PO Box 83
Andover MA 01810
tel. (508) 470-0840

Project Locations: Southwestern U.S.; Oro Grande, New Mexico; Kichpanha and St. George Key, Belize; and Cochabamba, Bolivia.

Project Types: Cave excavations, early Mayan village specialization, underwater archaeology of Little Spanish Armada, and early pottery and preceramic surveys.

Project Costs: Vary with project, but generally between $1,200 and $2,240 for two weeks. The more expensive projects are underwater ones.

Project Dates: Throughout the year at the various sites.

How To Apply: Write or call the above-listed office.

Work Done by Volunteers: Regular field and lab work at an archaeological excavation. Most volunteers work as partners with a field school student.

Special Skills or Requirements: No special skills are required, but an interest in archaeology is expected.

Commentary: The Andover Foundation for Archaeological Research was founded in 1984 by Dr. Richard (Scotty) MacNeish to provide opportunities for both students and interested amateurs to become involved in archaeological expeditions.

Sample Projects:

Kichpanha, Belize—excavation on the site of a small Mayan village that was occupied between 250 B.C. and A.D. 250, which was the beginning of the great Mayan civilization.

Fort Bliss, near Oro Grande, New Mexico—excavation of unlooted rock shelters of the Archaic Period, up to 6000 B.C.

21

Appalachian Mountain Club Trails Program
PO Box 298
Gorham NH 03581
tel. (603) 466-2721

Project Locations: In various national parks and forests, primarily in the Northeast, but some in Alaska, Wyoming, and Montana, plus out of several AMC lodges.

Project Types: Trail building and maintenance, many in remote locations.

Project Costs: Project fees range from nothing to $125, plus volunteers are responsible for all travel to project sites. Food, cooking and eating gear, and first aid supplies are furnished by AMC. Volunteers furnish all personal gear and camping equipment.

Project Dates: June through August for 10 to 12 days, with a few programs in the spring and fall. Volunteers can also arrange to participate on a weekend or for one or more weeks in addition to the 10- to 12-day projects. This is especially helpful for families and groups who want to work together.

How To Apply: Write to AMC Trails Program at the above address for an application and program brochure.

Work Done by Volunteers: Manual labor building trails.

Special Skills or Requirements: Volunteers should be in good health. Some backpacking experience is helpful, as is previous experience in trail building, although training in the use of tools and maintenance techniques is given at each project site. Minimum age is 16, with some younger participants accepted when accompanied by parents. Most volunteers are between 20 and 40 years old, but their ages range from 14 to 65+.

Commentary: AMC is the nation's oldest (organized in 1876) and largest (over 35,000 members) nonprofit conservation and recreation organization. It has 11 chapters in the Northeast, where it maintains over 1,000 miles of trails. The Trails Program is an extension of AMC's regular activities, and anyone may apply for participation.

Sample Projects: In recent years the AMC Trails Program operated projects in:

Kenai National Park, Alaska—continuing work on a new trail beside Exit Glacier.

White Mountain Wilderness, Lincoln National Forest, New Mexico—reconstructing and relocating portions of a trail.

Isle Au Haut, Acadia National Park, Maine—relocating a trail.

Amigos De Las Americas: Let the Youth Do It!

As I discuss volunteer vacations, whether with friends or with the media, no organization is greeted with more doubt than Amigos de las Americas. From national news reporters to local Sunday school teachers, almost everyone responds with skepticism as I relate how this organization sends youth, some as young as 16 years of age, into isolated Latin American villages where they become public health workers for the summer.

"Do you really mean to tell me that this organization lets these youth go into dangerous regions, and expects them to assume such terrible responsibilities?" is a frequent response.

In previous editions of *Volunteer Vacations* I have included a vignette that had some of these youth tell in their own words how they felt about their summers. For this edition I decided to tell about Amigos in words from an article written by Guy Bevil, Amigos founder, as the organization celebrated its 25th anniversary. In this article he wrote about the dream he and six other young men had in the mid-1960s, and how this dream has been fulfilled by almost 14,000 young people since 1965.

His dream began during the hot summer of 1964 in Honduras. During a vacation there, Guy Bevil visited many villages, and what he saw shocked him. Children were dying of communicable diseases when immunizations were available, at least in the U.S., so he asked one of the village mayors why. The sad response was quickly given. "Even God forgot this village, Señor Bevil."

As a youth minister in Houston, Texas, Bevil didn't forget it, and challenged the church youth and adults to help do something about the situation. As a result of those efforts, only eight cases of polio were reported during the fall of 1965 in the five provinces where he and 267 volunteers administered polio vaccinations earlier that summer. The number of cases across the rest of Central America reached epidemic proportions that fall. From that beginning came Amigos de las Americas.

How Did We Do It?

by Guy Bevil

As we celebrate our 25th anniversary, no one can be more surprised than I am. It was never my intention or that of any others that we should create a new agency. We started as Amigos de Honduras back in 1965, with serious questions about whether we could do everything we were committed to doing that summer. But we did it . . . and here we are! How did we do it? Why did we succeed where many others have failed? Three key principles in our success were:

We were willing to work where no one else would. When we went to the Minister of Health in Honduras, we said we wanted to work in the most abandoned areas, where no health service was available, where the government could not serve. Of course this created a credibility gap: they did not believe we were really willing to live in such places . . . and if we did, there was the question of whether we would survive. (That was one reason for the shorter terms in the early years.) Of course, we had to place some limits on work areas. We said we would go to the end of the road, plus four hours on foot or mule beyond. Often that was stretched by an hour or two, especially in the sixties.

We pointed out that working in these areas would protect the host government from any embarrassment in case of failure. "If we fail, no one will know it; if we succeed, you get all the credit." Who could resist an offer like that? This leads to the second factor in our success:

We did not seek acclaim for our work. We went with the attitude that the people of Honduras were doing something for us rather than reverse. They deserve the praise for trusting us, feeding us, and sheltering us. We didn't care who got the credit for our work. We discouraged honors. After the first year, when the government of Honduras gave me a medal, it was understood that no one could be recognized unless everyone was recognized, and diplomas became the accepted form of recognition.

We allowed young people to run the show in the field. From the beginning it was understood that the adults would run the program in Houston and the young people would run it in Honduras. What we were doing was so unique, there were no model programs to copy—we had to create an organization that would work without regular transportation or communication. Every day presented new challenges. Only young people could be flexible enough to face the challenges of overcoming major obstacles every day. And they did just that and are still doing it today. My own small contribution was to see the possibilities of matching the desperate needs in Central America with the boundless energy and idealism of American young people. It is still a winning combination.

Our final thought: *For Amigos to continue, we must keep trusting in our young people.* I keep hearing: "Times have changed . . . young people today are not idealistic . . . this generation is more materialistic." If you believe that, just talk to one of last summer's veterans. When we give them an opportunity to participate in the Amigos program, they come back and inspire us. As long as we hold to our original inspiration, we will not have to worry about the ongoing success of our organization. Our greatest risk will be that in doing such a good job, we may raise standards in Latin America to a point where we put ourselves out of business.

As part of the same 25th anniversary report on Amigos de las Americas that contained the above article, current president Margaret Guerriero wrote:

Guy Bevil started a dream in 1965 when he led 277 young people by plane and by truck caravan into Honduras. The dream became a reality when seven men put on paper the design of an organization. Kirby Atwood, Searcy Bracewell, Raymond Cook, Ed Frank, Jr., Ed Morris, Wilson Pais, and Jack Ripper incorporated Amigos de las Americas on November 4 of that year. From that day in November until today we have been defining both the dream and the reality.

Amigos volunteers have their baggage hauled by local transport as they arrive at their project site. (Photo courtesy of Amigos de las Americas)

The vision Guy had that young people were an untapped resource, capable of handling great challenges, was right. The vision, which Amigos has built and relied upon, is still valid today. The capacity to make good judgment calls, handle difficult situations, and shoulder incredible responsibilities has been proven every summer for 25 years by Amigos volunteers and field staff alike. I wish that everyone could watch as the field staff prepare for the summer project, are trained and then in turn are trainers, assess and negotiate a public health project in Latin America, and then work their way through tough problems during the summer. No other organization places so much confidence on the ability of youth. Amigos takes the leap of faith that young men and women can effectively carry responsibility that our society traditionally reserves for adults—and they do!

Appalachian Trail Conference

PO Box 807
Harpers Ferry WV 25425
tel. (304) 535-6331

Project Location: Volunteers are based at a rustic Forest Service lodge in Mount Rogers National Recreation Area in southwest Virginia. Trail Crews of four to six volunteers and a skilled leader will work on trails primarily south of Maryland on the Appalachian Trail. This work will be from Thursday to Monday, with a Tuesday/Wednesday weekend back at the base lodge.

Project Types: Heavy trail construction and land management projects.

Project Costs: Volunteers are responsible for transportation to Camp Konnarock. Once there, ATC and the Forest Service provide lodging, food, transportation, tools, safety equipment, and a small weekly stipend for laundry and incidentals.

Project Dates: Project begins in late May and ends in late August. Volunteers may sign up for the full season, part of the season (you choose how long), or a week.

How To Apply: Send for application to Appalachian Trail Volunteer Crew, c/o Appalachian Trail Conference, Southern Virginia Regional Office, PO Box 10, Newport VA 24128. Crews fill up quickly, so you should apply by January for the following summer.

Work Done by Volunteers: Work includes new trail construction, rock work, log work, shelter construction, and other physically demanding tasks.

Special Skills or Requirements: Must be 18 or older, although some experienced 16-year-olds may be accepted. Good health and enthusiasm are more important than previous experience.

Commentary: The Appalachian Trail is the longest marked footpath in the world, and America's first National Scenic Trail. It follows the crest of the Appalachian Mountains for more than 2,100 miles. The ATC is a private, nonprofit educational organization that coordinates public and private efforts to maintain and protect the Appalachian Trail. It joins hands with the U.S. Forest Service to operate the southern Appalachian Trail Volunteer Crew each summer. ATC also operates an August–October crew in the mid-Atlantic states.

Archaeological Excavations
PO Box 586
Jerusalem 91004, Israel
tel. (02) 292607; fax 972-2-292628

Project Locations: Throughout Israel.
Project Type: Archaeological excavation.
Project Costs: Registration fees range from nothing to $50. Volunteers generally are responsible for their own room and board, plus transportation to sites. Some sites offer accommodations, but require that volunteers pay for them. Volunteers must have their own accident and health insurance.
Project Dates: May through November, with vast majority between June and September. Minimum length of participation is generally one to two weeks, but some projects require more.
How To Apply: Apply to Archaeological Excavations at the above address. They will send a list of projects with individual information on each.
Work Done by Volunteers: Normal excavation work is done. This tedious and difficult work is made more difficult since volunteers must work long hours in hot weather.
Special Skills or Requirements: Requirements vary by project. Some require volunteers to have academic training in archaeology, while others accept volunteers as young as 16 and have no academic requirement at all. These are all spelled out in the yearly bulletin.
Commentary: These projects give volunteers an opportunity to learn firsthand about the early history of Israel while helping preserve this information for future generations.
Sample Projects: Some previous excavations were:
Jerusalem, Ein Yael-Emek Rephaim—an ancient farm with Middle Bronze Age and Roman and Byzantine remains.
Tel Mikne-Ekron—a large Iron Age site (twelfth to seventeenth centuries B.C.), which has been identified as Biblical

"Ekron," one of the five Philistine capital cities. Also investigation of intercultural connections between the Philistines, Israelites, Canaanites, and Assyrians.

Gamla—an ancient Jewish city that fell to the Romans in A.D. 67.

Archaeological Society of New Mexico

PO Box 3485
Albuquerque NM 87110

Project Location: Heaton Canyon, near Gallup, New Mexico.
Project Type: A field school that offers participants a chance to excavate at an archaeological site.
Project Costs: Tuition to field school is $50 per week, camping is available for $40 per week, and credit from the University of New Mexico is offered for $92 per unit.
Project Dates: Projects generally held in July.
How To Apply: Write to Phyllis S. Davis, ASNM, 3713 Camino Sacramento, NE, Albuquerque NM 87111, for information packet.
Work Done by Volunteers: Excavation and artifact curation.
Special Skills or Requirements: No special skills required.
Commentary: The ASNM Field School is small with limited facilities. This makes it impossible to accept any volunteers other than those enrolled in the field school. Since it is a nonprofit organization that receives no grants, it depends upon tuition for operational funds.
Sample Projects: Excavation of a Great Kiva and other structures from the Pueblo periods of A.D. 900 to 1150. Nearby sites are also being surveyed to determine the advisability of further excavations.

Arizona State Parks

800 W. Washington St., Suite 415
Phoenix AZ 85007
tel. (602) 255-4174

Project Locations: Throughout Arizona.
Project Types: Campground, interpretive, and visitor services hosts.
Project Costs: Volunteers are responsible for travel and living costs.
Project Dates: Year-round for varying lengths of stay. Campground hosts usually stay at least four weeks.
How To Apply: Send to Volunteer Coordinator at the above address for list of parks and application form.
Work Done by Volunteers: Campground hosts greet campers, assist with registration, give information about the park, and perform light park cleanup. Interpretive hosts conduct research and give visitors special information about natural or historical aspects of the park. Visitor services hosts provide park managers with assistance in a number of miscellaneous jobs as needed.
Special Skills or Requirements: Most positions just require a desire to volunteer.
Commentary: Most state and national parks depend upon volunteers to keep their parks presentable and interesting to visitors.

Association pour la Defense et L'Etude Canton de Levroux

Sophie Krausz
CNRS/ADEL
2, rue Traversiere 36
110 Levroux, France

Project Location: Chantier de Levroux.

Project Type: Archaeological excavation and restoration.

Project Costs: A 100-franc fee covers registration and insurance. Participants are responsible for transportation to site, plus room and board.

Project Dates: From early June to late August, with one-, two-, and four-week sessions.

How To Apply: Write to Sophie Krausz at the above address for application form and information. Don't expect English translations of brochures and applications, they just send their regular French forms.

Work Done by Volunteers: Manual labor on excavations and restorations.

Special Skills or Requirements: Must be 18 years of age and speak some French.

Commentary: This is one of several French projects that are using volunteers to restore medieval sites.

Bala Lake Railway

The Station, Llanuwchllyn
Bala, Gwynedd LL23 7DD, Wales
tel. 067 84 666

Project Location: Along the narrow-gauge railway.
Project Type: Railway restoration and operation.
Project Costs: Volunteers responsible for room, board, and transportation.
Project Dates: Railway operates between Easter and October, and volunteers are needed during entire season. Some volunteers are accepted off-season by prior arrangement.
How To Apply: Send a letter to Manager at the above address.
Work Done by Volunteers: All aspects of running and operating a small railway.
Special Skills or Requirements: Basic knowledge of trains is a plus, but there are plenty of basic maintenance and restoration chores available for those who have no prior experience.

Bristol Industrial Museum

Princes Wharf, City Docks
Bristol BS1 4RN, England
tel. Bristol 299771

Project Locations: At and near the museum.
Project Type: Restoration and running of working museum exhibits, most of which are steam-powered.
Project Costs: Volunteers are responsible for all living and travel costs.
Project Dates: Most weekends throughout the year.
How To Apply: Write to Andy King at the above address.
Work Done by Volunteers: Volunteers work as crew for an operating railway and a working steamship. They also do restoration work on a train and ship.
Special Skills or Requirements: Some knowledge of engineering principles is useful, but volunteers aren't tested.
Commentary: This is a small museum with a minimal budget that can use all the volunteers it can get.
Sample Projects: Crewing on the Bristol Harbour Railway, a dockside railway run by steam locomotives; crewing on the steam tug Mayflower, an 1861 steam-powered tug that now carries passengers; and working on the restoration of an 1878, 35-ton steam crane.

California Department of Parks and Recreation

PO Box 942896
1416 Ninth St.
Sacramento CA 94296- 0001
tel. (916) 445-4624

Project Locations: 67 campgrounds in state parks around the state.
Project Types: Campground hosts and camp interpreters.
Project Costs: Volunteer must furnish own trailer, camper, or mobile home. Campsites are free.
Project Dates: Year-round. Hosts must commit to a minimum of thirty days and work two to five hours per day. Interpreters make individual arrangements.
How To Apply: Write to one of the regional offices and specify whether you are interested in campground host or an interpreter position. The regions are:

Northern Region
3033 Cleveland Ave., Suite 110
Santa Rosa CA 95403-2186
tel. (707) 576-2185

Central Coast Region
2211 Garden Rd.
Monterey CA 93940
tel. (408) 649-2840

Inland Region
PO Box 1450
Lodi CA 95241-1450
tel. (209) 333-6901

Southern Region
1333 Camino Del Rio South, Suite 200
San Diego CA 92108
tel. (619) 237-7411.

Work Done by Volunteers: General campground host duties and specialized interpreter duties such as living history, environmental studies, and natural science programs.
Special Skills or Requirements: Must be at least 18 years old.

Liberia's First National Park

Liberia is not a wealthy country. Its people are fighting a war with poverty. And, as with many poverty-stricken countries in the Third World, rain forests are becoming casualties.

In the early 1980s Liberia's leaders recognized that they were in danger of losing a great natural treasure, and they designated their first national park in a virgin rain forest where no tourists, and few native Liberians, had ever been.

The 300,000-acre Sapo National Park, established in 1983, contains most of the mammalian species unique to the Liberian region. In the short time since the park has been formed, ornithologists have discovered two new species of birds and entomologists have identified several new species of dragonflies within its boundaries.

In a country where forests are disappearing rapidly—more than half have been clear-cut in the past 50 years, and more than 120,000 acres are lost each year—information on plant and animal life in the remaining virgin areas is desperately needed.

Foundation for Field Research is one of several organizations that are sponsoring projects attempting to determine the diversity of the park's species and population sizes.

Below is an article written for the foundation's newsletter by Ann Mcdowell, a film production assistant from Los Angeles and a volunteer on the first scientific expedition to work in the park.

My Journey into Africa

by Ann Mcdowell

Because of the Foundation for Field Research, I had the honor of being one of the first official visitors to the Sapo National Park in Liberia, West Africa. A group of four, we visited Sapo during the last two weeks of December 1987. Besides myself, the volunteers included a psychiatrist from New York City, and a recent retiree from AT&T who lives in Santa Barbara, California. Tom Banks of Foundation for Field Research accompanied us.

From the moment we set down at Robert's Field in Liberia, we were treated like VIPs. First, we were whisked through customs by Ale Peal, the co-principal investigator of the project and head of the park. Then we were given a police escort for the 45-minute ride into Monrovia, the capital of Liberia. In Monrovia we went straight to a press conference, complete with TV cameras. Fortunately, only Tom and Ale had to speak to the press. The rest of us were still numb from the trip and all the attention we were getting.

The next day we flew in a small plane, five passengers and the pilot, along the coast to Greenville, and made a perfect landing on a dirt airstrip. After lunch we were driven to the park guest house in Juarzon, where we met the Peace Corps volunteers working at the park, and Professor Nat Appleton (the other co-PI of the project), who would be going into the park with us. We were also properly introduced to Club beer, which is brewed in Liberia. The beer is very good and much more plentiful than soda. We went to bed early, knowing that we had a long, hot walk ahead of us.

Between Sapo Park and the main road is a buffer zone, at the edge of which is a Sapo tribal village. We stopped to pay our respects to the village leaders. We all sat under a tree, and the Sapo gave us their blessings and promises of protection (the official language of Liberia is English, but the Sapo spoke only their own language and used an interpreter).

After many photos, we left carrying their gift of a goat we named "Christmas Dinner."

From the Sapo village we were driven to the end of a logging road, where the trail into the park begins. There is only one way to get into the park: walking. Porters were hired to carry in our provisions and our bags. The porter who carried my bag also carried our alive-but-soon-to-be-chicken-dinner by the feet. The porters are so fast they go on ahead.

It took us three-and-a-half hours to walk from the end of the road to the Sinoe River, which is the park boundary. As with the trails inside the park, the trail leading to the river is well maintained with all the brush cut away, but it's still like a seven-mile obstacle course. At the river was a raft with someone to ferry us across. After that it was only a 30-minute walk to the camp. By the end we were hot, sweaty, and mighty proud of ourselves.

My main concern about the trip was snakes. Even though every other stick on the trail looked like one to me, only three real snakes were seen.

The camp is on Gbabany Creek, and consists of four buildings. The main building, where we slept, is concrete with a tin roof and four rooms. The other three buildings are used for storage and for the people who look after the camp. They are made in the native style, which is round, made of clay, and with a thatched roof. There is also a pit toilet and a bathing enclosure (a round, thatched screen about shoulder high). Most of our cooking was done in a fire pit in the middle of the camp. The Liberian help had their food cooked in a kitchen area near the creek. We had to have two cooking areas because we couldn't eat their red-pepper, spicy food, and they didn't care for our bland food.

The weather in the park was not what I'd expected or been prepared for. The first few days were hot and humid, but then we had rain and the nights turned cool. The days were warm and dry. Apparently this happens every year around Christmas, when the winds blow off the desert. I feel lucky that I was able to be in the jungle under such good conditions.

There was also a noticeable absence of flying insects. No

42

one had to use a mosquito net at night and the only time we were bothered was on the trails in the early morning. There was a large fly that would annoy the hell out of us, but as soon as we stopped moving, so did the flies. I guess I should also mention the river ants—they will swarm over and bite anything that moves. We also wore our socks up over our pants legs and constantly watched the person in front of us to see when they started hopping around like mad.

The park staff had built three platforms around the camp in areas of known animal activity, especially duiker activity. These observation platforms were constructed from small trees and placed five feet off the ground. One of the park rangers, who is an ex-hunter, would go to the platforms with us and give the call of an injured baby duiker. This usually brought either an adult duiker or animals of prey.

While sitting on the platforms I could hear so many birds, but I could rarely see them because they were in the thick canopy of leaves high above. One morning, while sitting on a platform near the creek, we could hear monkeys all around us. They sounded very close, but we couldn't see them through the thick vegetation. Suddenly they moved across a tree that didn't have any leaves. Apparently the monkeys then also saw us, because two climbed down a tree near us, took a good look, and scampered away. Before we left the platform we were able to see two more groups of monkeys. In fact, for the next two days the monkeys stayed in the camp area, and we were able to see them when we went out on the trails. One time they got right above us and shook the trees so that sticks, leaves, and fruit rained down.

Speaking of trails, there is nothing like coming off a hot jungle trail, having a few cold Club beers, and washing off with a warm bucket bath. To stand there and hear the birds as they go off to roost for the night, and to see the steam rise into the cool evening air, are truly some of life's finer pleasures.

And yes, I did mean cold beer. We had no electricity, except for bush current (full moon), but we did have a full-sized refrigerator that ran on kerosene. Four men hand carried it in on the same eight-mile trail we had walked.

Two of our days in the park were spent constructing another platform, a tree house 15 feet up, next to the Sinoe River. This one will be used for overnight stays to observe elephants and water buffalo. Robert, the ex-hunter turned ranger, was the master builder, and the rest of us helped by cutting down trees, hauling them to the construction site, and making rattan strips to bind it all together. No nails or tools other than a cutlass and saw were used. It will be finished off with a thatched roof and a plaque with our names.

We celebrated two holidays in the bush: Christmas and the New Year. We spent Christmas morning at the platforms, and Christmas afternoon roasting the goat. I don't think any of us missed all the hoopla that usually goes with Christmas in the States. Our Christmas trees were 100 feet high, and the lights were provided by fireflies. Instead of smoke from a house chimney, ours came from the cooking fire we sat around at night.

Volunteers observe wildlife from an observation platform in the trees of a tropical rain forest protected by the Sapo National Park in Liberia. (Photo courtesy of Foundation for Field Research)

New Year's Eve—well, I'm glad no one had to drive home. We didn't insist that everyone drink: only that everyone join us around the campfire at midnight. All but one did, and she ended up with a chicken in her bed. Neither was hurt, but neither would speak to us the next day. New Year's Day was slow . . . in anticipation of the walk out, of course.

The day after New Year's, we walked out. The walk went a lot slower than the walk in. We were able to get an early start, and we knew what to expect at the end of the trail. From Juarzon, we drove to Monrovia. (Future volunteers will fly back.) The drive was interesting but long: 12 hours long. We saw more of Liberia than most Liberians do.

While in Monrovia, we visited a biomedical research lab and talked with Dr. Agoramoorthy, who is in charge of rehabilitating chimpanzees in the wild. The highlight of the visit was going with him to one of the islands where the chimps had been released. Twenty to thirty chimps came running out of the island's jungle and were stopped short of coming out to our boat only by the deep water (chimps can't swim). Our boat held fruit and bread for the chimpanzees, which they caught as it was thrown to them.

Would I go again? Most definitely. But there are some other expeditions I would like to join first. In a few years, when Sapo Park has matured, I'll go back and say, "I knew it when . . ."

Foundation for Field Research volunteers dig, measure, and record artifact locations on an archaeological site on the island of Grenada in the West Indies. (Photos courtesy of Foundation for Field Research)

Canadian Bureau of International Education

85 Albert, Suite 1400
Ottawa, ON K1P 6A4, Canada
tel. (613) 237-4820

Project Locations: North America, Eastern and Western Europe.

Project Types: Workcamps where multicultural groups come together to assist local workcamps in completing needed local projects.

Project Costs: $125 application fee, plus round-trip transportation to project site.

Project Dates: Most workcamps are held between June and September.

How To Apply: Send to CBIE at the above address for complete application.

Work Done by Volunteers: Mostly manual labor. Building a playground, clearing hiking trails, or restoring a castle are just a few of the projects, but there are also some projects that are less physically demanding. Going on holidays with mentally handicapped adults, leading playground activities for neighborhood kids, or setting up a peace festival are a few of those. Most of these projects require 30 to 40 hours a week of work.

Special Skills or Requirements: Volunteers must be over 18 years of age, but there is no upper limit. Some projects require that volunteers speak French. CBIE only serves Canadian citizens. See listings for Council on International Educational Exchange and Volunteers for Peace for similar programs for U.S. citizens.

Commentary: CBIE is one of a group of worldwide organizations to participate in the international workcamp program. These projects have been popular for many years in Europe, and are now gaining more attention in North America.

Caribbean Conservation Corporation

PO Box 2866
Gainesville FL 32602
tel. (904) 373- 6441

Project Location: Tortuguero, Costa Rica.
Project Type: Marine turtle research.
Project Costs: $1,500 to $2,000 for 10- to 17-day expeditions, with all groups leaving from Miami.
Project Dates: March through September.
How To Apply: Write to the above address for application forms.
Work Done by Volunteers: Assisting researchers with sea turtle tagging operations as well as taking measurements and observing nesting habits.
Special Skills or Requirements: Good physical condition.
Commentary: This organization was formed in 1959 to support the work of the late Archie Carr, one of the world's foremost sea turtle authorities. Since then it has blended applied research and conservation projects in efforts to reverse the worldwide decline of sea turtles.

Casa de Proyecto Libertad, Inc.

306 E. Jackson, 3rd Floor
Harlingen TX 78550
tel. (512) 425-9552

Project Location: Harlingen, Texas.
Project Type: Legal work helping Central Americans with asylum proceedings.
Project Costs: Participants are responsible for all transportation, room, and board.
Project Dates: Summer is the busiest time.
How To Apply: Send resume and cover letter to the above address.
Work Done by Volunteers: Client interviews, case documentation, education, and advocacy work.
Special Skills or Requirements: Volunteers should be bilingual in English and Spanish, and computer skills are helpful.
Commentary: Because of the training involved, most projects need volunteers an entire summer, but there are special one-to six-week special projects as well.
Sample Projects: In addition to legal and educational projects, there are often fund-raising projects that appeal to special groups for money.

Chantiers D'Etudes Medievales

4, rue du Tonnelet Rouge
67000 Strasbourg, France
tel. (88) 37 17 20

Project Locations: Strasbourg and Viviers.
Project Types: Restoration of medieval sites and monuments.
Project Costs: 300–400 francs, which covers insurance, meals, and accommodations. Volunteers are responsible for transportation to sites.
Project Dates: July to mid-September, with 15-day sessions.
How To Apply: Send to Chantiers D'Etudes Medievales at the above address for application and information.
Work Done by Volunteers: Mostly manual labor, including excavation. There is an opportunity for volunteers to participate in the study of finds made during a dig. Volunteers work six hours per day, five days a week.
Special Skills or Requirements: Volunteers who aren't French must be at least 18 years of age, and should speak at least minimal French.
Commentary: For the past 15 years, 300–500 volunteers each year from over 20 countries have been divided into teams of 20 to 30 members to help excavate and restore medieval sites in France. While accommodations are neither fancy nor hotel-like, they are sufficient, and offer participants an opportunity to experience a true camaraderie with other volunteers.

The Charleston Museum

360 Meeting St.
Charleston SC 29403
tel. (803) 722-2996

Project Locations: In and around Charleston, South Carolina.
Project Types: Archaeological excavation on urban homesites
and rural plantations.
Project Costs: Participants must pay their own transportation
to Charleston and their own room and board while there.
Project Dates: Vary. Contact Martha Zierden, curator of historical archaeology, at the above address or phone for dates.
How To Apply: Write to Martha Zierden for application and
information.
Work Done by Volunteers: Volunteers work in both the field
(digging, screening, and measuring) and the lab (washing
and processing artifacts).
Special Skills or Requirements: Good physical health and ability
to withstand hard physical labor with heat and insects.
Commentary: Lab work is ongoing year-round, but excavation schedules are often unknown until one or two months
before the project begins. Most projects only last one to three
weeks.
Sample Projects: Excavations of various Georgian townhouses
and an ongoing excavation at a plantation site on Dill
Wildlife Refuge.

Cholsey and Wallingford Railway

Hithercroft Industrial Estate
Wallingford, Oxfordshire OX10 0NF, England
tel. Wallingford 35067 (weekends only)

Project Location: Along 2½ miles of track running from the above location.
Project Types: Restoration and maintenance.
Project Costs: None, but volunteers are responsible for all room, board, and transportation.
Project Dates: Weekends year-round.
How To Apply: Contact the above address for more information.
Work Done by Volunteers: General railway restoration and maintenance.
Special Skills or Requirements: None but the ability to do heavy work.
Commentary: This is entirely a voluntary organization.
Sample Projects: Clearing vegetation from track right-of-way, restoring railway cars, and providing general maintenance.

Christian Medical/Dental Society

Medical Group Missions
PO Box 830689
Richardson TX 75083-0689
tel. (214) 783-8384

Project Locations: Projects are ongoing in Africa, the Philippines, Jamaica, the Dominican Republic, Central America, and Ecuador.

Project Types: All projects are medical or dental.

Project Costs: $375 per person, plus airfare to project site.

Project Dates: Projects are held throughout the year for two weeks, except for those in Africa, which are for three weeks.

How To Apply: Send to the above address for application form and list of projects.

Work Done by Volunteers: All work is medically oriented. Physicians do their specialty and are generally supported by two nurses. About one-third of the volunteers are nonmedical personnel who act as support workers for the medical volunteers.

Special Skills or Requirements: Medical training for nurses, dentists, and physicians, but only a desire to help for others.

Commentary: There are great contrasts between the various projects. In some countries the living conditions and medical facilities are very primitive, while others, such as Mexico and Jamaica, offer semiluxurious (dorms or small cottages for families) accommodations. This is one of the few medical volunteer organizations that welcome entire families. However, they do prefer that any children be in their teens, or close to it.

Christian Ministry in the Parks

222½ E. 49th St.
New York NY 10017
tel. (212) 758-3450

Project Locations: Volunteers serve in 65 national parks and recreation areas across the country.

Project Type: Christian service to employees and visitors of the parks.

Project Costs: Volunteers pay their transportation to and from the parks, but receive room and board plus a small stipend for the summer.

Project Dates: June 1 through Labor Day.

How To Apply: Send to the above address for application and information.

Work Done by Volunteers: Leading worship services and bible studies, directing choirs, and pursuing other ministerial duties.

Special Skills or Requirements: A commitment to the Christian faith, creativity, maturity, and the ability to work with Christians of all denominations.

Commentary: This program is for single students and married couples over 20 years old who wish to spend a full summer working in one of our national parks ministering to the religious needs of others. Volunteers should be either seminary or college students with special skills in music, bible study, recreation, drama, or Christian education.

World Beyond Our View

by Anne Marcotty

I took a long run down the beach this afternoon. The scenery here is fantastic. Ilha do Cardoso is a small but mountainous island, heavily forested with (so far) at least two different types of forest. The surrounding islands and the mainland are also quite mountainous, with jagged, jutting peaks, softened only slightly by their dense forest cover. I've never seen anything like it. They look as though they are new mountains, like those in Arizona or Hawaii, but Tim Moulton says that they're pre-Cambrian (back when trilobites were the wave of the future). Mountains that old should have softened by now.

When I was running—through what felt like bathwater—a thunderstorm came up fast from the west. The air and sky were filled with varying densities of water vapor, making gray and silver curtains that reflected the light and turned the mountains into different shades of teal and blue. The whole world, it seemed, was silver and green and blue and luminous.

Day 2

We went frog hunting tonight. This served two main purposes. One was to start the task of censuring the island to determine what species are here, in what concentrations, and in what relationships with other critters. The other reason was to get our feet wet (literally) for field biology. We spent the day carrying drift-net traps through the forest and up the mountain, placing them at strategic locations along the way. Arduous work, but I'm determined not to be a whiner, and by God, I am going to be an expert frog finder if it kills me. Right about now, it feels like it will.

One thing that won't come out in the photos is the sound of the jungle, especially at night. I think that the only thing missing is a good bass sound. Everything else is represented well—the textured and varying high-frequency buzz and hum and chirp, the staccato clicking and percussive "hammering," the melodic fluting, the trills and whoops and whir-

Collecting tadpoles on a frog-hunting expedition. (Photo courtesy of Anne Marcotty)

ring of wings, and even what sounds like laughing. There's hooting and whistling and crying and a fruity warbling sound. But no bass notes.

The night jungle is fragrant beyond description. There are many flowers that open at night. Since it's dark, they don't need to spend energy on showy blossoms, so they have more energy and need for a scent that attracts pollinators. This is an intense, magical, sexy, and fecund place. It is so fecund, in fact, that several barbed seeds attached themselves to me on our walk into the forest, and by the time we walked out, they had sprouted.

Day 3

Today I held my first caiman. It was a young, small male that we were processing for tagging and release. Jay got in the tank to catch him. The tank was filled about shin-deep, and the beast was crouched in a shaded corner. Jay was able to grab him around the throat and tail and pin him to the bottom of the tank while he got a better grip. Then he pulled him up. The caiman was only about a meter long, but they are much stronger than we are, and their teeth are a force to be reckoned with. The crocodile wriggled and twisted for awhile, then calmed down. Though I was worried about not being strong enough to hold him, I couldn't pass up the opportunity to do so. It was a heady moment when I took hold of this cool, writhing, muscular bundle of primal urges. It's electrifying to hold something so alive and yet so alien. There is nothing superfluous on this small, intense creature. He has all of our senses—sharp color vision, hearing beyond anything we can imagine, a strong sense of smell and taste, perfect teeth, and beautiful skin. He has no fat—all the stored energy goes to length, and he'll grow to a length of three meters. His kind have been around unchanged since the early Cretaceous, 130 million years ago, and without human meddling, they probably will outlast us.

Our fieldwork tonight—another frog hunt—was mercifully cut short by more rain than I've ever seen. It hadn't rained for two days, and the lightning was flashing almost constantly, creating a strobe effect over the nighttime jungle. The usual orchestra was hushed but for an occasional peeping and the ominous backdrop of thunder. Here at last were the bass notes that had been missing earlier. Then the rain came. We were only a half-mile from camp, but because the soil is mostly clay and doesn't absorb, we were wading by the time we got back. I couldn't have been wetter if I'd taken a shower. I kept laughing in total surrender to the rain.

Day 6

This morning we climbed up to a cave and had lunch. It was obvious from the smell that cats had been there. That's the closest we'll get to seeing a jaguar, although I keep hoping to before I leave. To my artist's eye, a jaguar is the crown jewel of the jungle. But, I'm told, a cat is just a cat. Besides the obvious size and coloring differences, a jaguar is very much like a tiger or a cougar or a lion—or my own cats, for that matter. They eat, reproduce, sleep, and socialize in much the same way from species to species. The jungle heavyweight champs as far as natural histories go are the frogs and lizards and insects. They're the ones that have adapted bizarre mating rituals, odd appendages, curious digestive systems, and developed ways of perceiving the world that we'll never even guess at. I'm finding that beauty, to a field biologist, can be found in the muck and slime. I am thankful for this new way of seeing.

Anne Marcotty was a volunteer on an Earthwatch Island Rain Forest expedition in 1990. This article was originally published in Earthwatch Magazine.

Christian Movement for Peace

427 Bloor St. West
Toronto, ON M5S 1X7, Canada
tel. (416) 921-2360

This is another organization that offers volunteer opportunities through the international workcamp movement. It
is the Canadian counterpart of Volunteers for Peace in the
U.S.

Club du Vieux Manoir
10, rue de la Cossonnerie
75001 Paris, France

Project Locations: Three permanent sites—Guise, Argy, and Ponipoint—and 12 to 15 other sites throughout France.

Project Type: Restoration of ancient monuments and sites.

Project Costs: 45 francs for membership and insurance for one year, plus 45 francs per day for room and board. Participants are responsible for transportation to and from site. Participants must bring all personal sleeping, eating, and toilet gear. Summer accommodations are in tents, often with very rustic facilities (i.e., no running water at many sites).

Project Dates: There are no set dates for the three permanent sites, but all other sites operate only during the summer months. Volunteers stay a minimum of fifteen days, with new sessions beginning on the second and sixteenth of each month.

How To Apply: Send to Secretary, Club du Vieux Manoir, at the above address for application form and brochure.

Work Done by Volunteers: Normal manual labor of a restoration project. Volunteers are required to accept the demands of project supervisors or they will be asked to leave.

Special Skills or Requirements: Excellent health and a willingness to do hard physical labor are primary requirements. The club is open to everyone over the age of 13 from all nations, with no maximum age limit. Preorganized groups are welcome.

Commentary: These projects aren't "something to while away spare hours." As the club's brochure states, ". . . they are aimed not at the consumer but at the enthusiastic volunteer who wants to do something worthwhile."

College Cevenol International

Work Camp Admissions Office
c/o Bill Brown, Work Camp Admissions Officer
Box 68170
Brown University
Providence RI 02912
tel. (401) 272-5158 or (401) 751-2169

Project Location: The campus of College Cevenol in Le Chambon-sur-Lignon, France.

Project Types: Vary according to the needs of the college. Can be anything from remodeling to woodworking to painting.

Project Costs: $125, which includes room, board, and insurance. Volunteers are responsible for all transportation and spending money.

Project Dates: Early part of July for 3½ weeks.

How To Apply: Write to Bill Brown at the above address for application form and brochure.

Work Done by Volunteers: Manual labor on projects defined by college. Volunteers follow a regimented schedule with wake-up at 7:00 A.M. each day, with breakfast followed by work until noon. There is another two-hour work period after the lunch break. This is followed by free time, language course work, and seminars. Dinner is at 7:00 P.M., and evenings are free.

Special Skills or Requirements: This program is for students between the ages of 17 and 25 who have had at least two years of high school French. Only eight Americans are chosen to participate in the program each summer.

Commentary: Volunteers live in rustic, barrack-like dormitories, eat simple but hearty French country food, and work hard in a mountain environment with 20 to 25 other volunteers from 6 to 8 different countries.

Colonial Williamsburg Foundation

Department of Archaeological Research
PO Box C
Williamsburg VA 23187
tel. (804) 220-7330

Project Locations: The restored area of Williamsburg, Virginia, the eighteenth-century capital of the Virginia colony.

Project Type: Archaeological field and laboratory work.

Project Costs: Vary from projects where volunteers are responsible only for transportation, room, and board, to those where out-of-state participants in the College of William and Mary Field School pay approximately $1,800 for a five-week session.

Project Dates: Vary, but summer field school usually runs from June to September.

How To Apply: Send a query letter to the above address.

Work Done by Volunteers: Tasks related to daily excavation (troweling, recording, screening soil) and laboratory processing of artifacts (washing and numbering).

Special Skills or Requirements: No experience or special skills are required for most positions, but volunteers must have the physical ability to perform excavation tasks.

Commentary: There are three different programs offered through the foundation. The first is the field school of the College of William and Mary. Participants in this program must register through the college for at least one five- week session. They need have no background in archaeology and will receive six semester units of credit for the session. The second program is Learning Weeks in Archaeology, where participants enroll in one- or two-week sessions, and are introduced to the goals and methods of the research program at Williamsburg. The third is for individual volunteers who have some background in archaeology. Participants in this program help with the excavation and laboratory work under minimal supervision, and can choose the time and length of their stay.

Colorado Trail Foundation

548 Pine Song Trail
Golden CO 80401
tel. (303) 526-0809

Project Locations: Colorado national forests.
Project Types: Trail building and maintenance on the 470-mile Colorado Trail.
Project Costs: $25 registration fee.
Project Dates: June, July, and August, with both weekend and week-long projects.
How To Apply: Write to the above address for summer trail crew schedule.
Work Done by Volunteers: Trail building and maintenance and trail signing.
Special Skills or Requirements: Good health and a willingness to work. Foundation provides experienced leaders and tools.
Commentary: Foundation sets up base camps for volunteers and provides food. Volunteers provide their own sleeping bags, tents, and personal items.
Sample Projects: The Colorado Trail is a 470-mile trail stretching from Denver to Durango. It was built (and continues to be improved) largely by a massive volunteer effort.

Commission on Religion in Appalachia (CORA)

450 N. Kneeland Dr., Box 608
Richmond KY 40475
tel. (606) 623-0429

Project Locations: 90 workcamps in the Appalachian states of Pennsylvania, Ohio, Maryland, West Virginia, Virginia, Kentucky, Tennessee, North Carolina, South Carolina, Georgia, and Alabama.

Project Types: Workcamp groups for home repair, small farm development, and similar projects.

Project Costs: Vary with project, but generally between $100 and $150 per person.

Project Dates: Projects are done in spring and summer.

How To Apply: Apply as a group to John MacLean, Coordinator of Volunteers, at the above address. List number of people in your group, ages, and preferred dates (for week-long workcamps).

Work Done by Volunteers: Home repair including activities such as plumbing, painting, weatherization, and other general home repair projects.

Special Skills or Requirements: CORA prefers to have one or two skilled craftspersons with experience in home repair in each group.

Commentary: CORA only accepts groups for workcamps, and only groups of 8 to 30 people should apply. Groups are usually adult/youth church or college groups, and should apply by January for spring or summer assignments.

Sample Projects:

Crossville, Tennessee—several youth groups helped build a new house.

London, Kentucky—church youth group insulated and paneled a two-room home.

Harlan, Kentucky—college group did construction, housepainting, and cleaning.

St. Paul, Virginia—college group dug new water line, hauled wood, and cleared garden.

Committee for the Health Rights in Central America

347 Dolores St., #210
San Francisco CA 94110
tel. (415) 431-7760

Project Location: Nicaragua.
Project Type: Health colloquium and medical teaching exchange.
Project Costs: $1,200 to $1,300.
Project Dates: Usually in February or November for 10 days.
How To Apply: Write to the above address for registration information.
Work Done by Volunteers: Medical teaching exchange in six hospitals in Nicaragua, as well as attendance at colloquium.
Special Skills or Requirements: Must be health care workers, health professionals, or interested in community health projects.
Commentary: Task force of participants investigates the delivery of health care in Nicaragua.

Community Service Volunteers

37 Pentonville Rd.
London N1 9NJ, England
tel. 071-278-6601

Project Locations: Throughout the United Kingdom.
Project Type: Working the elderly, physically disabled, mentally ill, homeless, and others who need help living independently.
Project Costs: About $500 for the summer program, plus travel to and from the U.K.
Project Dates: May through September for 10 to 16 weeks.
How To Apply: Write to the Overseas Programme at the above address.
Work Done by Volunteers: Face-to-face work with those in need, in both group and individual situations.
Special Skills or Requirements: No experience or special skills are needed, except ability to speak and understand English.
Commentary: CSV operates a nonrejection policy for volunteers. The organization feels that anyone who wishes to volunteer has something to offer. They also offer a program that requires a four- to twelve-month commitment.

Medical Missionary Experience in Ecuador

by Kent Mellerstig, M.D.

Family vacations are a common feature of life in the United States. And the pictures we carry in our minds of these experiences often match scenes from *National Lampoon's Vacation* or *European Vacation* with Chevy Chase. But there are other "movies" to be lived out, namely, those involving travel in foreign countries.

Last summer, my family and I traveled south of the American boarder to Ecuador on a medical missionary tour. The group we went with was the Medical Group Missions, a program sponsored by the Christian Medical/Dental Society.

This group offers the opportunity to go to an underdeveloped country to offer medical assistance to the poor and needy, plus a way to be a U.S. ambassador of goodwill. Because this is a Christian group, it offers the additional opportunity to share Christian love and concern.

Yes, the tour was organized. But it was not your run-of-the-mill, senior citizen bus tour. There were 55 people in our group, including 10 teenagers, 8 physicians, several dentists, 14 nurses, interpreters, and general helpers. And yes, we went on vacation—not to relax, but to work. We did not go across the country in a green station wagon. Instead, we went through the Andes in Ecuador, South America—descending 8,000 feet from the springtime climate of Quito at 9,500 feet to the semitropical heat of Santo Domingo, at 1,500 feet—in

67

Frederick Edwards, M.D., works on an assignment in south Africa with the medical services program of Direct Relief International. (Photo courtesy of Direct Relief International)

two Mercedes buses driven by drivers who enjoyed chasing each other, playing chicken, and passing gasoline trucks around blind corners. Our destination was not Wally World, but the area around Santo Domingo de los Colorados. There the surgical team worked at a 140-bed hospital that served a population of 300,000. Two other clinical teams went to a number of rural villages.

The surgical facilities at Domingo de los Colorados were surprisingly excellent. And, amazingly enough, the local physicians had offered to suspend their elective surgical schedule for the two weeks that we were there. I can not imagine this happening at any hospital in Sonoma County, for any visiting medical group from anywhere in the world.

The supervisor of the operating room was a Roman Catholic nun who ran a very tight ship. There was an excellent attempt at sterile technique, using one gurney from the floor and another gurney in the operating room. And although we had attempted to bring as many surgical supplies as we could, we still had to depend on their generosity. For example, it was virtually impossible to bring enough surgical scrubs, as we wanted to include a number of our team who had never been in an operating room. Hence, we practically overwhelmed the laundry. The scrub suits were washed and

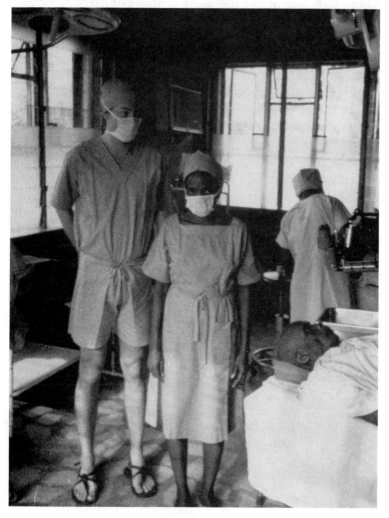

A Focus, Inc. volunteer and an African nurse and patient take a break from eye surgery. (Photo courtesy of Focus, Inc.)

pressed—by hand, I assume—in a hot, uncomfortable dungeon in the lower bowels of the hospital by people we never met and never had the chance to thank for making it possible for us to help their fellow countrymen.

While there, we performed 24 plastic surgical procedures from cleft lips and cleft palates to burn scar contractures. There also was about the same number of orthopedic and urological cases. My secretary, Sue Johnson, who was helping us in the operating room, had very wisely brought along a number of stuffed animals that she gave to each child at the conclusion of the operation. And it was a toss-up as to which they appreciated more, the surgery or the stuffed toy.

The teams who went to the outlying villages focused on providing dental care, mainly in the form of dental extractions. The medical focus was on treatment of parasite and other tropical diseases; the team saw approximately 150–200 patients a day, including Ecuadorians, and Colorado and Chicua Indians.

The fascination of the trip was not only the work but, primarily, the people with whom we spent time. Another important aspect was the unparalleled opportunity to share an unusual side of medicine with our children. My son Jason

A home for volunteers staying in Ecuador.
(Photo courtesy of Kent Mellerstig)

Kent Mellerstig, M.D. (right) and Ecuadoran assistants.
(Photo courtesy of Kent Mellerstig)

was able to spend two weeks as a dental assistant while my other son, Dean, had the chance to be an interpreter. They both had the chance to go to the operating room and observe an operation in progress.

The boys also had the broadening opportunity to see a number of teenagers from Ecuador, some of whom were along as interpreters, and most of whom had, shall we say, Communistic leanings. Although Ecuador is not embroiled in internal strife to the extent that many Latin American countries are, the signs of dissent are there. The teenagers also criticized the United States for buying their products, such as bananas, inexpensively and exporting expensive manufactured goods. This reminds me of what Japan is doing to us.

A medical project like this is organized with the help of the local evangelical Christian missionaries. The service that we provided also is a goodwill gesture for the local church.

Quite often, North American Christians have romanticized missionary life in a foreign country. This no doubt originates in our childhood memories of visiting missionaries who came on furlough bringing stories and paraphernalia from strange countries. I remember vividly, as a young child, hearing a wife of a missionary introduce her husband as having been in Tanganyika for so long that he had forgotten how to speak English. And being so young, I actually believed her for a few minutes until he started to speak English.

In view of this, it was exciting to meet the missionaries in their own surroundings. One English lady had been working as a missionary with the Colorado Indians for 40 years, while the missionaries we met in Quito were using the latest technology in running one of the world's largest radio stations, HCJB, the voice of the Andes. It was a unique experience to attend a live HCJB radio production that was beamed to North America for direct broadcast and a delayed broadcast to Asia and Europe. The program included a performance by a violinist who plays with the Quito symphony. The HCJB group also has one of the most respected hospitals in Quito, the Voz Andes Hospital. The missionaries in Ecuador are, indeed, multitalented and hardworking individuals.

If one thing became symbolic to me of the U.S. relationship to an underdeveloped country, it occurred when we, a group of eight, chartered a bus. The reasons for doing so were very logical. First, it is dangerous to drive in the country if you are not from Ecuador. Second, a rental car is very expensive and there were no Hertz or Avis agencies nearby. And the only alternative for the eight of us was public transportation, which meant riding packed together, unable to communicate well, with a lot of people with uncertain schedules, in a foreign country. Thus, for $100 a day—the same amount one could pay a cardiologist to work four hours per day for a month—we rented a large bus.

I am sure you can understand why we made the wise decision to charter the bus. The local residents, however, probably questioned our choice. In a country such as Ecuador, most of the population depends on buses for transportation. The major roads are well paved and many people live along them. Thus, many people stand by the roadside to flag down a bus. But our bus never stopped. Nor did we request the bus driver to stop for anyone. It was an uncomfortable experience. I could not help but wonder what these people thought of a large empty bus going by and not stopping.

Another local custom was the lack of a 25-mile-per-hour speed limit in towns. Hence, the bus driver would barrel through as fast as possible, blaring his horn at any pedestrian

Before and after shots of an Ecuadoran girl who had surgery on her palate. Medical Group Missions volunteer Kent Mellerstig, M.D., performed the surgery. (Photo courtesy of Kent Mellerstig)

or bicyclist that strayed in his way. Some of the towns showed signs of never-to-be-finished construction projects and political graffiti painted in red with prominent hammer and sickle, as well as signs saying "Yankee Go Home." One of the missionaries interpreted the true meaning of the sign to be "Yankee Go Home But Take Me With You."

Of course such experiences raise in my mind the question of why our country is so wealthy when there are other countries that are so poor. And certainly, we as U.S. citizens are not personally responsible for our own good fortune. Yet there seems to be very little inclination for some of us to share significantly with the very poor.

In retrospect, the rewards and exhilaration of traveling in a Third World country and sharing medical skills under less than ideal circumstances outweigh the conventional "pleasures" of many a family vacation. I would urge you and your family to take a medical group mission vacation. It will certainly enrich your life, give you a different perspective, and no doubt cause you to be more thankful and more appreciative at home.

Dr. Kent Mellerstig has practiced as a plastic surgeon in Northern California since 1974. This article was first published in the Sonoma County Physician, *Santa Rosa, California.*

Companheiros Construtores

Rua Pedro Monteiro, 3-1
3000 Coimbra, Portugal

Project Locations: Throughout Portugal.
Project Type: Home construction and repair, plus a few social service projects.
Project Costs: Transportation to and from project, plus spending money while there. Volunteers may have to pay for room and board.
Project Dates: Short-term projects are for two to three weeks during the summer months.
How To Apply: Send to Manuel Rocha, Companheiros Construtores at the above address for information.
Work Done by Volunteers: Hard manual labor on projects for the poor of Portugal.
Special Skills or Requirements: Willingness to work. Construction skills are desirable. Some social service projects need specialized skills such as physical therapy.
Commentary: This is a small organization that does much good work in Portugal, with occasional projects in other European countries. Few Americans have worked as volunteers, but they are welcome. They also are in need of financial support for their program.
Sample Projects: A recent project involved building a small home for a family from Angola who had been evicted from the shed they were living in. The father was sick and unable to work, and the mother could only find temporary jobs.

Concordia

27, rue du Pont-Neuf, B.P. 238
75024 Paris, France
tel. (1) 42 33 42 10

Project Locations: Alpes, Auvergne, Bourgogne, Midi-Py-renees, and Thierache regions of France.

Project Types: Protection of environmental and architectural heritage.

Project Costs: Registration fee of 450 francs. Food and lodging provided.

Project Dates: From March to December, for one to three weeks.

How To Apply: Contact the above office.

Work Done by Volunteers: Volunteers work for six hours a day, five days a week on a wide variety of construction and renovation jobs.

Special Skills or Requirements: Volunteers must be 18 years old or above, and in good physical condition. Some knowledge of French helpful.

Commentary: Some projects are concerned with modern building projects and camp maintenance, while others are involved with the restoration of medieval villages and structures.

Sample Projects: Improving a footpath by clearing, cleaning, and constructing signs; improving a youth center by renovating the roof and masonry; restoring the framing and roofing of a Roman chapel; and renovating an old hamlet by restoring stairs that go to the ramparts.

Connecticut State Office of Parks and Recreation

165 Capitol Ave.
Hartford CT 06106
tel. (203) 566-2304

Project Locations: Campgrounds in various state parks and forests.

Project Type: Campground hosts.

Project Costs: None.

Project Dates: Memorial Day weekend through Labor Day weekend.

How To Apply: Send to the above address for application and job description.

Work Done by Volunteers: Volunteers must be available for a minimum of four weeks and will serve as the live-in host of a campground. Their primary responsibility is to assist campers by answering questions and explaining campground regulations. Light maintenance work may also be performed. Volunteers are expected to work weekends and holidays, but different hours can be arranged with individual park managers.

Special Skills or Requirements: Volunteers must be neat, courteous, and willing to meet the public. They should also have a knowledge of state park programs and regulations.

Commentary: This is one type of volunteer work where volunteers are encouraged to bring their families.

Costa Rica National Park Service
—Volunteer Program

Aptdo. 10104-1000, Av. 6 y 8, C. 25
San Jose, Costa Rica
tel. 33-45-33; fax 23-69-63

Project Locations: National Parks of Costa Rica.

Project Types: Park maintenance and environmental education to help protect national parks.

Project Costs: Participants must pay for transportation to site and food while there ($4 per day).

Project Dates: Projects ongoing year-round, with a minimum of three weeks required of volunteers. This time can be spent at more than one park. Volunteers are used at Tortuguero, Cabo Blanco, Poas, Braulio Carrillo, Irazu, Guayabo, and Tapanti.

How To Apply: Write a letter to the above address with dates you are available, and include a brief personal history stating what knowledge or skills you have that may be useful to park service.

Work Done by Volunteers: Volunteers have constructed trails, provided tourist information, gathered garbage, cooked, fought forest fires, weeded, and much more.

Special Skills or Requirements: No special skills are required, but artistic skills and the ability to do manual labor are helpful.

Commentary: It is important that volunteers be able to work in a tropical climate, and in challenging conditions. When you apply you may suggest the park or type of climate in which you want to work. The park service will attempt to comply with your requests. Specific information on the work location and conditions will be provided in the service's reply to your application.

Cotravaux

11, rue de Circhy
75009 Paris, France
tel. (1) 874 79 20

Project Locations: Primarily in France, but Cotravaux is associated with workcamps in other countries.
Project Types: Workcamps dealing with recreation, environmental protection, historic restoration, etc.
Project Costs: Vary by project, but generally minimal.
Project Dates: Year-round.
How To Apply: Send to the above address for brochure and application form. Be prepared; they only send publications in French, as do many French volunteer organizations.
Work Done by Volunteers: Varies by project, but most require physical effort.
Special Skills or Requirements: None.
Commentary: Cotravaux doesn't organize workcamps, but it helps obtain volunteers for the 77 association members.

Council for British Archaeology

112 Kennington Rd.
London SE11 6RE, England
tel. 01-582-0494

Project Locations: Throughout the United Kingdom.
Project Type: Archaeological excavation.
Project Costs: Volunteers are responsible for travel, room, and board, plus some tuition costs for training excavations.
Project Dates: Excavations are held throughout the year, but volunteers are used primarily between April and October.
How To Apply: Read about advertised projects in the *British Archaeological News,* and apply directly to projects.
Work Done by Volunteers: General excavation work.
Special Skills or Requirements: No special skills are required for most digs, although some require previous excavation experience.
Commentary: The CBA does not organize projects, but advertises projects organized by others. Subscription to its newsletter is $25 per year (six issues) for air mail, and $16 for surface mail.

Council of International Programs

1030 Euclid Ave., Suite 410
Cleveland OH 44115
tel. (216) 861-5478

Project Locations: Various European countries and India.

Project Types: Programs for professional social and youth workers.

Project Costs: All participants must pay travel expenses to the project location. Some projects cost up to $500 for registration, while others cost nothing. Room and board is generally provided by the host program.

Project Dates: Various times during the year for four to eight weeks.

How To Apply: Send to the above address for more information.

Work Done by Volunteers: Supervised fieldwork in host country.

Special Skills or Requirements: Many projects require language fluency, and all require experience and training in youth or social work.

Commentary: CIP has been facilitating exchanges for human services professionals for over 30 years and has over 6,000 alumni from 120 countries.

Council on International Educational Exchange

205 E. 42nd St.
New York NY 10017
tel. (212) 661- 1414

Project Locations: Eastern and Western Europe, North Africa, and North America.
Project Types: Conservation, construction, archaeology, historical renovation, and work with children.
Project Costs: $125 application fee, plus transportation, insurance, and spending money while on project.
Project Dates: From late June to early September.
How To Apply: Send to CIEE at the above address for application and information bulletin. Initial application should be made by late February or early March to insure placement. Application deadline is April 15.
Work Done by Volunteers: Manual labor, social work, and playground supervision. May include painting, digging, working with tools, planting and weeding, or visiting with disabled people.
Special Skills or Requirements: Must have a desire to do hard work in a multicultural setting and a sense of adventure. Must be at least 18 years of age on most projects.
Commentary: This is one of the major workcamp organizers in the U.S., plus they offer many other programs for travel and study abroad.
Sample Projects: In recent years, volunteers have been involved in the following: forest conservation in Czechoslovakia and the U.S., care of the elderly in West Germany, construction of a water trench in Turkey, renovation of historic sites in France, and archaeological digs in Spain.

The Mendenhall Ministries: A Rural Christian Community Development Organization

The volunteer coordinator for the Mendenhall Ministries wrote, in an issue of their newsletter, about the call of the volunteer, and about the importance of volunteers to the various projects in their ministry.

He noted that during the first nine months of 1988, 14 groups and 18 individuals, totaling almost 200 volunteers, contributed more than 8,000 hours of volunteer labor to help improve the lives of the poor of Mendenhall, Mississippi.

One of those volunteers was Marilyn Shaver of Walnut Creek, California, who volunteered with a group from the Walnut Creek Presbyterian Church. After she returned from Mendenhall she wrote the following article for the Mendenhall Ministries' newsletter.

Learning My Neighbor

by Marilyn Shaver

"Why did you come to Mendenhall as a summer volunteer?" was a question I was asked during my visit at the Mendenhall Ministries. I had trouble giving a simple response because it was a question I had been turning over in my mind for sometime. My response at that moment was: "I came as a member of a team from Walnut Creek Presbyterian Church in Walnut Creek, California. I want to live and work for two weeks in a holistic Christian community

Marilyn Shaver relaxes on some of the lumber used to renovate homes. (Photo courtesy of Marilyn Shaver)

development." Each day God continued to give me new insights about why I was there.

It was some 10 years ago when I first heard the name Mendenhall. I read the book *Let Justice Roll Down*, by John Perkins, and was deeply stirred by his works describing what life was like for some people living in Mendenhall. I left with a burning question: How could anyone return to a community that had treated them so badly? John often referred to "living on the other side of the tracks." I wondered how I would feel if I had to live in a community set apart and labeled the "quarters."

I learned more this past spring when Dolphus Weary

spoke to a group of us in California. As he told the story of the Good Samaritan my heart filled with compassion, and I was challenged by another question: Who is my neighbor?

Now, because of this summer, the people of Mendenhall have become my neighbors. Each day I met individuals who had been living with no hope and now know the power of the Lord. These are people who have learned to carry the burden by leaning on Jesus. I see love in action as a variety of people with different gifts reaching out and reconstructing dilapidated houses, helping adults learn to read, caring about the legal rights of the poor, providing jobs, and going out to discipline people of all colors and races. I understand in Christ we can make a difference together.

As our van crossed the railroad tracks for the last time, I looked back and read the sign, "Mendenhall Bible Church—Abundant Living Through Jesus Christ." I laugh as I think about God's sense of humor, sending a person from an affluent area to a rural community in order to learn the principles of being a good neighbor and discover the reality of abundant living through Jesus Christ. Dolphus Weary said, "Your neighbor is anyone God puts you into contact with." My personal challenge as I returned to California is to live each day with my eyes open to whom God sends my way.

About a year after Marilyn Shaver and her group worked in Mississippi, the volunteer coordinator for The Mendenhall Ministries wrote the following article about another group of volunteers.

Volunteers: More Than Fair-Weather Friends

In Mississippi, when it rains, it pours, and you hope that you have a good roof over your head. If you don't, then you better get out the pots and pans to catch the drips.

Back in March, we heard about an elderly gentleman who was living in an old house with a bad roof. He had saved for many months to buy some tin for a new roof, but was unable to do the work. He suffers from diabetes and related physical problems, and it was a nurse caring for him that called to see if we could help. She had contacted some government agencies for help, but to no avail.

When the call came to us for help, there was a group of volunteers here already hard at work on several projects. Before the week was up, some of those volunteers went out to reroof the old man's house only to discover that there was only enough tin to cover about half the house.

There was no money to buy any more tin, and the volunteer group had to return home, but they were not content to let it go at that. They pitched in and mailed us some money to buy more tin, and with the help of some more volunteers, the old man has a good roof over his head when those Mississippi rains come pouring down.

Not all the stories surrounding the experiences of volunteer groups are as heartrending as this one, but every group has made an important contribution to our efforts to minister to the poor.

Cousteau Society

930 W. 21st St.
Norfolk VA 23517
tel. (804) 627-1144

Project Locations: Various remote areas of the ocean.
Project Types: Ecological and scientific explorations.
Project Costs: $2,000 to $3,000, plus transportation to departure site.
Project Dates: Generally held during summer months.
How To Apply: Send to Project Ocean Search, Cousteau Society, at the above address for an application form and brochure. You can call (213) 656-4422 on the West Coast for information only.
Work Done by Volunteers: Collecting and organizing specimens and other samples for a project that is in progress.
Special Skills or Requirements: Although diving is not a requirement, it is strongly recommended for full participation in projects. Participants who wish to dive on the project must bring their own equipment and proof of national certification. A medical examination is required to confirm physical fitness, especially for those who are diving.
Commentary: Jean-Michel Cousteau participates in each Project Ocean Search expedition, along with a team of scientists and guest faculty members who are specialists in the area being studied. These expeditions are closer to study tours than they are hard-core scientific expeditions, but participants are involved in very worthwhile projects in small groups (groups are limited to 35 on most expeditions).

The society emphasizes that those who attend Project Ocean Search are paying participants, not volunteers who attend free of charge.

Cross-Lines Cooperative Council

1620 S. 37th St.
Kansas City KS 66106
tel. (913) 432-5497

Project Location: Kansas City.
Project Types: Home repair on low-income housing.
Project Costs: Participants pay $8 per night.
Project Dates: June through August, with length of stay three to five working days.
How To Apply: Contact Work Group Coordinator at the above address.
Work Done by Volunteers: General home repair from replacing broken windows to reroofing and rebuilding foundations.
Special Skills or Requirements: Carpentry skills are preferred but not necessary.
Commentary: The council attempts to get groups of 5 to 20 people of high school age or older together to work on needed projects.

Crow Canyon Archaeological Center

23390 County Road K
Cortez CO 81321
tel. (303) 565-8975 or (800) 444-8975

Project Location: Southwestern Colorado, near Mesa Verde National Park.

Project Types: Archaeological excavation and environmental archaeology.

Project Costs: Adults, $690 per week; college students, $420 per week; and high school students (field school), $1,600 for four weeks.

Project Dates: End of May through mid- October.

How To Apply: Write to the above address or call Dottie Sanders on the 800 number.

Work Done by Volunteers: Excavation, lab analysis, and long-range studies of plant communities.

Special Skills or Requirements: No special skills are required, aside from the usual manual labor of excavations.

Commentary: Participants make a significant contribution to Crow Canyon's archaeological research.

Cultural History Council

PO Box 462
Cayucos CA 93430
tel. (805) 772-0117

Project Location: Clear Lake Basin in northern California.

Project Type: Archaeological excavation.

Project Costs: Volunteers are responsible for transportation to and from site, and for tuition fees which vary from year to year depending upon donations received by the council.

Project Dates: Generally for one week throughout July and August.

How To Apply: Send resume to Cultural Heritage Council at the above address. There deadline for the July program is May 1.

Work Done by Volunteers: Archaeological site preparation, grid layout, excavation, and lab work.

Special Skills or Requirements: Volunteers not enrolled in a field school course offered by the council must have at least two seasons of archaeological field and/or lab work.

Commentary: Field school courses for high school and college students as well as for other adults are offered in field and lab methods, and an introductory course in archaeology is offered for junior and senior high school students.

This program has been conducted since 1983, and the study of a 10,000-year-old Pomo Indian village has resulted in a collection of more than 4,000 artifacts that have been excavated and cataloged.

Dart Valley Railway Association

The Railway Station, Buckfastleigh Station
Devon TQ11 0DZ, England
tel. 0626-64596

Project Locations: Buckfastleigh, Totnes, and Paignton and Kingswear railways.
Project Types: Restoring and operating as support for the railways.
Project Costs: None, but must provide own room and board.
Project Dates: Continuous throughout the year.
How To Apply: Write to the association at the above address for application materials and dates of current projects.
Work Done by Volunteers: All aspects of railway work.
Special Skills or Requirements: None required, but some positions may only be available after special training.
Commentary: Applicants must join the DVRA and obtain work permits for insurance purposes.
Sample Projects: Recent projects include maintaining and running a station, rebuilding a station from scratch, and restoring locomotives and carriages to working order.

Dean Forest Railway Society

Norchard, Lydney
Gloucestershire, England
tel. 0594-413423

Project Locations: Lydney to Parkeno.
Project Types: Restoration of four miles of railway line and running of steam trains on weekends from May through September.
Project Costs: Annual membership in the society is 6 pounds. Volunteers may apply for a weekly rate of 1 pound.
Project Dates: Restoration work is year-round, and trains run during the summer.
How To Apply: Write to Volunteer Coordinator at the above address for application forms and information.
Work Done by Volunteers: All work involved in the operation of the railway is done by members of the society who want to volunteer.
Special Skills or Requirements: The responsible jobs of running the trains require training and testing, but there are many maintenance, painting, and other manual labor jobs that require minimal training, which is given on the job.
Commentary: A limited number of beds in railway coaches (bring a sleeping bag) are available for volunteers. Although there are no cooking facilities there are numerous eating places a mile away in Lydney. The Forest of Dean is an ancient ironstone and coal-mining area of considerable interest to industrial archaeologists. It now has beautiful deciduous and pine forests full of wildlife.
Sample Projects: Painting a railway coach inside and out, building a dry stone wall, and assisting in a shop or restaurant are all examples of volunteer work.

Dental Health International

847 S. Milledge Ave.
Athens GA 30605
tel. (404) 546-1715

Project Locations: Cameroon, Nigeria, El Salvador, Cook Islands, Bhutan, and Zambia.

Project Type: Creating rural dental clinics and installing U.S.-made equipment donated by U.S. dentists.

Project Costs: Airfare and in-country transportation to and from work site.

Project Dates: Volunteer opportunities are available year-round.

How To Apply: Telephone DHI between 7:00 and 10:00 P.M. eastern time, Sunday to Thursday.

Work Done by Volunteers: Collecting and installing dental units, assisted by local plumbers/electricians, and teaching specialties.

Special Skills or Requirements: All volunteers must come from the upper 50 percent of their graduating classes, be members of ADA, and be in excellent physical health.

Commentary: Dental students and dental hygienists are also asked to apply, but all who apply must realize this is back-breaking work in an inhospitable environment. Dr. Barry Simmons, founder and president of DHI, has often screened more than 1,200 patients in a day, while giving some type of treatment to more than 100.

Direct Relief International

Attn: Colleen Silvestri
PO Box 41929
Santa Barbara CA 93140-0820
tel. (805) 687-3694

Project Locations: All over the world where people are in need of medical care.

Project Types: Short- and long-term medical and dental projects at hospitals and other medical facilities.

Project Costs: On short-term assignments volunteers are responsible for all their travel expenses. The host facility generally provides room and board for the volunteer, and often for other family members. These accommodations will usually be very basic, however.

Project Dates: Short-term assignments are for a minimum of four weeks, and may be at any time of the year.

How To Apply: Send to Direct Relief International, attn: Colleen Silvestri at the above address for a list of currently available assignments and application form.

Work Done by Volunteers: Volunteers provide clinical assistance as requested by the host facility, and often help teach and train local staff members.

Special Skills or Requirements: Volunteers must be professionally qualified in one of the many medical and dental specialties, and prepared to work where facilities and training may be far below what professionals are accustomed to in the U.S. The program needs volunteer physicians, dentists, nurses, physical therapists, medical technicians, dental hygienists, pharmacists, and other health professionals.

Commentary: It isn't always possible for DRI to match volunteers with their location preference, but every effort is made to find an assignment for everyone who volunteers. DRI acts as an intermediary between facilities who have stated a need for volunteers from the U.S. and other countries. This means that it often takes some time to arrange a volunteer project, so keep that in mind when you contact them.

Guatemala: The Highlands

In the lush and temperate central highlands of rural Guatemala, people struggle to make their lives a little bit better. Workers there average about $800 a year, and many can't read or write. But they have loving, vibrant extended families, stable communities, and tremendous hope for their future and their children.

Merle Hebeisen of Hopkins, Minnesota, had expected the residents of the central highlands to be filled with futility and hopelessness, but, as she wrote after her trip as a participant in a Global Volunteers' project there: "Instead I found a

A Global Volunteers participant helps build furniture in Guatemala. (Photo courtesy of Global Volunteers)

strength of the human spirit to carry on in spite of limited circumstances; an attitude of innovation and 'let's make-do with what we have'; friendliness and kindness from the people; eagerness to learn new ideas; (and) hope for their children to have a better life than they've had. I'll keep memories of the beauty of Guatemala, its mountains, volcanoes, flowers, exotic fruit trees—papayas, mangoes, bananas—as well as the heat, humidity, and the comfort of clean water and a porcelain toilet back home."

The majority of men in the central highlands farm or work as laborers. Women assume roles critical to their families' survival: carrying water from the river, collecting wood for fuel, grinding corn, making tortillas and cooking meals, and caring for the young children.

Many of those children attend the primary school. In two of the villages where Global Volunteers projects have been located, the youngest boys and girls go to a community-operated preschool. Some teenagers go to the secondary school in Sanarate, but many must help their parents with farming and other family duties.

The schools these children attended were very different from those of Wadpole, New Hampshire, where Elizabeth MacLachlan lived; they had none of the modern equipment or glossy materials, but, she reported, "Being with the kids was so interesting, because I saw that they were just like little kids anywhere in the world. It's good to know that we all start out the same. I thought I'd feel sad and sorry for the people, but they have so much that we don't have, like the sense of family and community."

MacLachlan saw that there was hope in both the children and their parents, and this gave her hope for their future.

Over the past several years, Global Volunteers teams have worked alongside the people of the villages of Llanos de Morales, Monte Grande, and San Miguel Conacaste. Volunteers from across the United States, such as Hebeisen and MacLachlan, have contributed their time, energy, and creativity to helping villagers in a variety of development projects such as renovating an old building into a preschool

A volunteer joins in with a local seamstress on a Global Volunteers project in Guatemala. (Photo courtesy of Global Volunteers)

and preparing and assembling toddlers' tables and chairs, constructing and painting a community center, building an addition to an elementary school, and installing a system for potable water. Other activities have included analyzing crop diseases, teaching English, coaching volleyball, organizing aerobic exercises, helping preschoolers use toothbrushes, painting murals, and providing assistance to develop small businesses.

Larry Beans of Moraga, California wrote that he and his wife "didn't want a typical tourist vacation. We wanted an adventure. I wanted to give to people with personal involvement." And that is what he and other volunteers have experienced with Global Volunteers. During their two-week visit to a village, teams of eight to ten volunteers stay at a church annex, a community center, or a rented house. A local woman cooks food for the volunteers over a gas plate and wood fire. In the evening, team members report on the day's work and adapt the schedule for the remaining time.

While working with the villagers, the volunteers have

discovered a new understanding of the men and women of this small Central American country. Faces have names and strangers become friends. Local families join the team at evening meals to visit, and often invite volunteers to their homes for tea, or to community celebrations. Volunteers learn firsthand of the villagers' hopes, dreams, values, and struggles.

The teams also spend a few days outside the villages. Sites to visit include the old capital of Antigua, one of the most affluent cities of the New World in the seventeenth century. The ruins there reveal a rich Guatemalan history, and Indians have set up shop to sell their unique handmade crafts. In Guatemala City, the breathtaking Nation Palace and the central market provide fascinating insights into the country's history and economy.

These visits to sites away from the villages where they are working give volunteers an opportunity to learn about the history of Guatemala in addition to experiencing firsthand the lives of its people today.

Combined, these experiences give volunteers a new look on their own lives as well as on the lives of those who had previously been strangers. After returning from her trip Deborah Howard of Minneapolis, Minnesota wrote, "Each moment of each day was filled with newness—with an opportunity of a new perspective or new outlook on life. . . . My mind has been opened to a whole new way of thinking. It's a great thing to have our minds jostled from time to time."

And Melissa Rhoads of Dallas, Texas wrote, "I once felt sorry for the people in developing countries, but now I feel hope and more empathy rather than sorrow. My own values were changed in a very positive way, one in which I truly experienced the reality that material things don't make a person happy. I'm much more relaxed and comfortable with the true understanding that I can live a tremendously full life without a great deal of money."

Global Volunteers' need for volunteers continues to grow as more and more villages ask for their involvement. Volunteers don't need to speak Spanish to be productive. Anyone with a willing heart and the desire to lend a hand can make a contribution.

This article was adapted from material written by Bud Philbrook, Global Volunteers president, for the organization's newsletter.

Earthwatch

680 Mount Auburn St.
Box 403N
Watertown MA 02272
tel. (617) 926-8200

Project Locations: In 1990, Earthwatch sponsored 120 projects in 46 countries and 22 states.

Project Types: 28 of these expeditions were in art and archaeology; 41 were in life sciences; 14 in geoscience; 12 in rain forest ecology, and 4 in social studies.

Project Costs: In 1990, costs ranged from $695 to over $2,000, with an average of $1,300. Volunteers are responsible for round-trip transportation to the staging site.

Project Dates: Projects are conducted year-round. Volunteers join expeditions for two- to three-week stints.

How To Apply: Write to Earthwatch at the above address for membership information, expedition application, and catalog of expeditions and team dates. Membership is $25 per year and includes six color magazines describing projects.

Work Done by Volunteers: Varies according to scientific discipline of project, but expedition leaders (all university professors) expect volunteers to be flexible and follow expedition guidelines.

Special Skills or Requirements: Most expeditions require no special skills, only a willingness to work and learn. When special skills are needed (scuba, photography, etc.), they are noted in the magazine and expedition briefing. Volunteers who have special skills such as surveying, birding experience, nursing training, etc., are always welcome.

Commentary: Founded in 1971, Earthwatch sponsors scientific field research by finding paying volunteers to help scientists on their projects. In 1990 more than 3,000 volunteers, who ranged in age from 16 to 83 and came from every profession and background, helped on over 550 teams. The mission of Earthwatch is to improve human understanding of the planet, monitor global change, conserve endangered habitats and species, explore the vast heritage of our peoples, and foster world health and international cooperation.

Sample Projects: A few of the many expeditions that Earthwatch has offered recently are:

Sandy Point, St. Croix, U.S. Virgin Islands—leatherneck turtles were measured, tagged, and examined, and thousands of eggs were rescued from erosion.

Sarasota Bay, Florida—the 100+ resident dolphins in this natural laboratory were netted, marked, and noted for age, sex, paternity, and social interaction.

Los Tuxtlas Biological Preserve, Vera Cruz, Mexico—the effects of rain forest destruction and fragmentation were examined by recording flora and fauna in some of Mexico's last fragments of rain forest.

Queensland, Australia—koalas were observed by quick capture and release, and vegetation of habitat was examined as a food source and habitat requirement.

Montana, U.S.—volunteers helped find fossil evidence of what killed the dinosaurs—was it an extended "winter" or global warming that caused their extinction?

San Juan Island, Washington—volunteers helped document by photo the 80+ orcas in the area to determine how humans impinge on their lives and livelihood.

Ecology Center

1403 Addison
Berkeley CA 94702
tel. (415) 548-2220

Project Location: Berkeley, California.
Project Types: Community outreach, newsletter production, environmental issue research, etc.
Project Costs: None, but volunteers are responsible for all transportation and living costs.
Project Dates: Year-round.
How To Apply: Contact Naomi Notman at the Ecology Center.
Work Done by Volunteers: Quite diverse—projects are tailored to individual volunteers, but all are in keeping with the center's role of offering alternatives to the public on environmental issues.
Special Skills or Requirements: None, but public relations skills and an interest in the environment are helpful.
Commentary: This is a community-based environmental education center that advocates changing many of our consumer-oriented policies to help protect our environment.
Sample Projects: Updating and authoring fact sheets on subjects such as recycling, organic gardening, or styrofoam; staffing tables at fairs; maintaining an environmental and recycling data base; staffing office phones; and doing mailings.

Farm Hands—City Hands

Green Chimneys, Putnam Lake Rd.
Brewster NY 10509
tel. (914) 279-2995, ext. 202

Project Locations: A large number of farms in the northeast.
Project Type: Farm work.
Project Costs: Vary with project.
Project Dates: Farm Days are held throughout the year, and placements for extended stays are based on applicants' and farmers' needs.
How To Apply: Send a self-addressed, stamped envelope to the above address.
Work Done by Volunteers: Everything from making maple syrup to flower planting to making wine and cheese.
Special Skills or Requirements: Most special skills are taught by the farmers, but you do need to be in excellent health and able and willing to work long, hard days.
Commentary: This program was begun to educate and involve city dwellers about farms and farmers, and most of the placements are on for-profit farms, although most are small and specialized. Many volunteers are interested in organic farms and produce and are placed on such farms.

One nonprofit farm that accepts volunteers is the Green Chimney Farm School, a private residential school that focuses on farming.

Ffestiniog Railway Co.

Harbour Station
Porthmadog, Gwynedd LL49 9NF, Wales
tel. Porthmadog 2340

Project Locations: The mountains of Snowdonia in Wales.
Project Types: Wide variety of work projects on a working steam railway.
Project Costs: Volunteers are responsible for transportation to the project, and room and board at the site. There are several self-catering hostels nearby where accommodations are reasonable.
Project Dates: Volunteers are welcome year- round.
How To Apply: Send to Volunteer Resource Manager, Ffestiniog Railway Co. at the above address for information brochure and application form. The information brochure lists the many types of volunteer opportunities available.
Work Done by Volunteers: Every aspect of railroading is open for volunteers although some, such as locomotive operator, require that the volunteer spend considerable time gaining experience.
Special Skills or Requirements: Previous experience working on a railroad is always desirable, but a willingness to learn is all that is required.
Commentary: The history of the Ffestiniog Railway goes back to 1836, and some of the steam locomotives and coaches still in use are over 100 years old. The railroad reached its peak in the last decades of the nineteenth century, with a general decline after that until it was closed down in 1946. In the early 1950s a group led by Alan Pegler reopened the line as a nonprofit organization operated with the assistance of a voluntary society. Part of the line reopened in 1955 with other parts opening periodically until the line was completed in 1982. Today it is the busiest independent railway in Great Britain, and is run by the oldest railway company in the world, since it was originally incorporated in 1836 by an act of parliament, and required a new act to abandon the rail-

way. Since such an act was never passed, the original company is still in existence.

Florida Department of Natural Resources

Division of Recreation and Parks
2900 Commonwealth Blvd.
Tallahassee FL 32399
tel. (904) 488-8243

Project Locations: State parks throughout Florida.
Project Types: Campground hosts and general volunteer duties.
Project Costs: None.
Project Dates: Vary.
How To Apply: Contact the above address for names of individual parks and park managers and apply directly to the park managers.
Work Done by Volunteers: Primary work is as campground host, assisting campers in park campgrounds, monitoring activities in the campground, and helping to maintain campground facilities.
Special Skills or Requirements: Clean appearance and the ability to work with people.
Commentary: Campground hosts volunteers for six to twelve weeks, and volunteers must be available in campground for three hours each day, and for four nights each week.

Florida Trail Association

PO Box 13708
Gainesville FL 32604
tel. (904) 378- 8823

Project Locations: Throughout Florida.
Project Types: Trail maintenance, development, and footbridge building.
Project Costs: Minimal, mainly travel to work sites.
Project Dates: Year-round trail work.
How To Apply: Membership in FTA insures notification of work schedule.
Work Done by Volunteers: Trail building and maintenance activities.
Special Skills or Requirements: None, but volunteers should be in good physical shape and willing to do manual labor.
Commentary: Most participants are FTA members, and membership is open to anyone.

Focus, Inc.

Department of Ophthalmology
Loyola University Medical Center
2160 S. First Ave.
Maywood IL 60153
tel. (708) 216-9598

Project Location: Nigeria.
Project Types: Ophthalmology, medical and surgical.
Project Costs: Volunteers are responsible for all transportation, plus about $1,700. Room and board are furnished at the site.
Project Dates: Projects run year-round, with volunteers serving for one month.
How To Apply: Write to Focus, Inc., Department of Ophthalmology, Loyola University Medical Center, at the above address for application and information.
Work Done by Volunteers: Eye surgery.
Special Skills or Requirements: Must be certified ophthalmologists.
Commentary: Most assignments are now used to staff year-round a clinic in Abak, Cross River State, Nigeria.

Food First
(Institute for Food and Development Policy)
145 Ninth St.
San Francisco CA 94103
tel. (415) 864-8555

Project Location: Home office in San Francisco.

Project Types: Vary.

Project Costs: Volunteers are responsible for their own travel and living costs.

Project Dates: Positions of varying lengths are available year-round.

How To Apply: Contact Frederico Gil-Sola at the above address or phone.

Work Done by Volunteers: Research for specific IFDP books, or programs and clerical work in various departments.

Special Skills or Requirements: Volunteers should be responsible, self-motivated, organized, and independent. Computer skills are always welcome, but not necessary.

Commentary: Food First is a center for research and education for action. Their mission is to stimulate increased public education and citizen participation in solving critical social problems locally, nationally, and globally. They seek to free people from myths that deny hope and block action against hunger, poverty, and other social problems.

Sample Projects: Past volunteers have worked on updating Food First publications, entering information into data base, writing instruction manuals, and coordinating Reality Tours. Specific openings are always changing.

Canada's Native Gardening Project

The Mennonite Central Committee—Canada began their Native Gardening Project in the mid-1970s to return to America's native communities a gift they originally gave us: the gift of gardening.

Because of the disruption of the native culture in most communities in Canada, much of the knowledge of gardening that had been passed on to the early immigrants has been lost. There is now a need to return this gift and help

Participants in an orientation for the Mennonite Central Committee—Canada's Native Gardening Project. This group later moved to various Native American communities in Canada for the summer to help reintroduce productive gardening techniques to Native Americans.
(Photo courtesy of Len Siemens)

110

A Native American harvests lettuce from a garden that was developed with the assistance of Mennonite Central Committee—Canada volunteers. (Photo courtesy of Mennonite Central Committee—Canada)

reintroduce productive gardening techniques to Native Americans.

The Mennonite Central Committee Native Garden Project started almost 50 gardens in Native American communities during the past decade, and almost 200 volunteers have served with the project. In 1987, 20 communities requested volunteers in remote areas of the Yukon, the Northwest Territories, British Columbia, the Prairie provinces, and Ontario.

Kate and Lily, two recent volunteers in the Native Garden Project, wrote the following in their diary during their summer:

It was fun planting with the people. They are always complaining about how the children pulled out last year's carrots. One five- year-old asked his mother where the carrot row was and she refused to tell him for fear of what he may do during his spare time. But in most of the gardens where we worked children were eager to help. Sometimes the rows were crooked or the potatoes and onions were planted upside down, but we enjoyed the enthusiasm the children generated.

We finally got rain—two days of it! Hopefully now the gardens will grow.

The people have been most friendly and we have felt very welcome. Kate and I lived with a family for the first two weeks, but now we have our own lovely home. How encouraging when people stop by and give us moose meat, dried or fresh, and fish. It makes us feel accepted and glad to be here.

We went duck hunting with the family that hosted us. When we returned home, duck cleaning became a family affair. Even the five-year-old participated, thoroughly enjoying the de-feathering. What impressed me most was that the parents didn't tell the children how to clean the ducks. The children just watched, then imitated the parents. The things that draw a family closer!

With planting out of the way, we can now involve ourselves in other activities. We hope to start a cooking course with some of the women. Several of the men who hope to study carpentry need help with math. As the summer progresses I'm sure we will find other things to do. And if we get bored, there is always the weeding that needs to be done.

Foundation for Field Research

PO Box 2010
Alpine CA 92001-0020
tel. (619) 445- 9264

Project Locations: Projects are located worldwide.

Project Types: Scientific research expeditions.

Project Costs: From $200 to $1,800, and volunteers are responsible for round-trip travel to the assembly area, although the foundation does make travel arrangements. There are some scholarships available for students and teachers.

Project Dates: Projects are held throughout the year.

How To Apply: Write to Foundation for Field Research for current brochure and application.

Work Done by Volunteers: Wide variety of research project assistance. Every expedition the foundation supports is chosen because of it needs and can use nonspecialist help.

Special Skills or Requirements: Some projects require special skills such as scuba certification, but most have no special requirements. The foundation looks for people who are willing to become active members of the research team, working alongside the scientist and helping to fulfill the expedition's goals. On-site training in field techniques is given to volunteers.

Commentary: Foundation for Field Research unites researchers' needs with the members' support. The public subsidizes research projects by volunteering their help to scientists in the field, and by contributing a tax-deductible share of the cost of the projects.

Sample Projects: Below are some sample expeditions:

Primate Census in Liberia, Africa—identifying and observing monkeys in a virgin tropical rain forest.

Prehistoric Cultures of Grenada—assisting with the survey and excavation of Arawak and Carib Indian sites on the island of Grenada, West Indies.

Romanization of Southern Italy—working on the excavation of a town from 200 B.C. that survived the Punic Wars.

Project Prairie Dog—observing and census-taking of prairie dogs along the Missouri River in Montana.

Giant Leatherbacks of Michoacan—moving eggs from nesting sea turtles to a nursery area and help tag sea turtles as they come ashore.

Desert Archaeological Survey—surveying for prehistoric sites in Anza Borrego State Park, California.

Foundation for International Education

121 Cascade Ct.
River Falls WI 54022
tel. (715) 425-2718

Project Locations: Worldwide, but mostly in English-speaking countries.
Project Type: Working as an elementary or secondary teacher alongside a regular teacher.
Project Costs: Between $330 and $400, plus accommodations and travel expenses.
Project Dates: For three weeks, mostly during the summer months, but occasionally during winter.
How To Apply: Write to Dr. Ross Korsgaard at the above address for information.
Work Done by Volunteers: Assist regular classroom teachers with their usual duties.
Special Skills or Requirements: Should be an experienced, credentialed teacher.
Commentary: Accommodations are generally quite inexpensive, as volunteers normally stay with one of the teachers on the school staff.
Sample Projects: Volunteers have served in England, Scotland, Ireland, New Zealand, India, and Australia since this program started in 1972.

Four Corners School of Outdoor Education

East Route
Monticello UT 84535
tel. (800) 525-4456 or (801) 587-2859

Project Locations: The Four Corners states of Utah, Colorado, Arizona, and New Mexico.

Project Types: Educational and research programs on the natural and human history of the Colorado plateau region.

Project Costs: Projects vary in cost from $275 to $1,395.

Project Dates: Between February and November.

How To Apply: Send to the above address for brochure and application forms.

Work Done by Volunteers: Archaeological documentation, surveying, and digging.

Special Skills or Requirements: No special skills, just an interest in the subject matter.

Commentary: While this program has many educational classes that don't involve volunteer work, it also has a number of archaeology and natural history projects that utilize volunteers.

Sample Projects: In the past years projects have included an archaeological documentation project of Anazazi ruins along the shores of Lake Powell; an archaeological excavation near Dolores, Colorado, and a peregrine falcon survey of the San Juan River and Dark Canyon Wilderness Area.

Frontiers Foundation—Operation Beaver

2615 Danforth Ave., Suite 203
Toronto, ON M4C 1L6, Canada
tel. (416) 690-3930

Project Locations: British Columbia, Northwest Territories, Alberta, and Ontario in Canada, plus Haiti, Sierra Leone, and Senegal.

Project Types: In Canada most projects have been either building or renovating homes and community centers, although recently there have been some projects in cold-weather agriculture. These all involve joint community-volunteer efforts. Volunteers are also used in both the National and regional offices, plus some short-term overseas positions when one of the overseas projects has special manpower needs such as graphics, medical, or secretarial that aren't available locally.

Project Costs: Cost varies by project. Contact Operation Beaver for more information.

Project Dates: Agricultural and building projects are primarily in the summer, with two-month commitments. Short-term positions are developed as needs arise and volunteers become available. The length of these varies according to the needs of both the foundation and the volunteer.

How To Apply: Send to Frontiers Foundation—Operation Beaver at the above address for information brochure and application.

Work Done by Volunteers: Broad variety of construction and agricultural work, plus some office and clerical work.

Special Skills or Requirements: Willingness to work hard in a cross-cultural setting. Helps to have previous construction experience, but that isn't required.

Commentary: Operation Beaver was begun in 1964 as an ecumenical workcamp by the Canadian Council of Churches, and the Frontiers Foundation assumed responsibility for the program in 1968. In its first 25 years, 2,250 volunteers from 60 countries and 17 North American Indian Nations helped build or renovate almost 1,400 homes, 24 community training centers, 3 greenhouses, and a cold-climate agriculture station. This program is an excellent example of the cross-cultural workcamp concept.

Genqtur Turizm ve Seyahat Acentasi

Yerebatan Cad. 15/3 Sultanahmet
34410 Istanbul, Turkey
tel. (90-1) 526 54 09

Project Locations: Throughout Turkey.
Project Type: Workcamps.
Project Costs: Registration fee plus travel and personal expenses.
Project Dates: Two to three weeks from late June through early September.
How To Apply: Send to the above address for information, or ask about Turkish workcamps through one of the voluntary workcamp organizations in U.S.
Work Done by Volunteers: General manual labor.
Special Skills or Requirements: Generally none, but any that are necessary are printed in annual brochure.
Commentary: This organization also organizes inexpensive study tours and Turkish language courses.
Sample Projects: Between 15 and 20 different workcamps are operated each summer, and a new archaeological dig in central Anatolia has just been organized.

Global Volunteers

375 Little Canada Rd.
Little Canada MN 55117
tel. (612) 482-1074

Project Locations: Jamaica, Guatemala, Tanzania, Western Samoa, India, Paraguay, Mexico, Poland, and Vietnam.

Project Types: Construction, teaching, public health, business consulting, agriculture, etc.

Project Costs: Vary from $1,075 to $3,000.

Project Dates: There are 36 two- to three- week projects throughout the year.

How To Apply: Contact the above office for application form.

Work Done by Volunteers: Tutoring local school children, painting and constructing homes and public buildings, or laying pipe for water system, all in cooperation with local villagers.

Special Skills or Requirements: No special work skills required, but a willingness to share, learn, and work alongside others are all part of the effort.

Commentary: Volunteers from all ages, professions, and backgrounds join together on teams on these projects to live in rural villages by invitation to help raise their standard of living. Some predeparture training is provided by Global Volunteers.

Gloucestershire Warwickshire Railway

Toddington Station
Toddington, Gloucestershire GL54 5DT, England
tel. 024269-346

Project Locations: Near the towns of Toddington and Winchcombe.
Project Type: Reconstruction of a mainline railway.
Project Costs: Membership in the society at 6 pounds per year, plus own room and board.
Project Dates: Every weekend.
How To Apply: Write to Membership Secretary at the above address.
Work Done by Volunteers: Tracklaying, building, and locomotive and carriage restoration.
Special Skills or Requirements: None, but they will attempt to fully utilize any special skills volunteer has.
Commentary: The railway is in beautiful countryside with a view of the Cotswolds on one side and the Vale of Evesham on the other. The ancient villages of Didbrook and Hailes can also be seen from the tracks.

Great Western Society Limited

Didcot Railway Centre
Didcot, Oxfordshire OX11 7NJ, England
tel. 0235-817200

Project Location: Didcot.
Project Types: Normal railway restoration and maintenance.
Project Costs: Approximately 5 pounds per day for food.
Project Dates: Work week is the first week of August each year. Other times are available by appointment.
How To Apply: Write to the above address for application and information.
Work Done by Volunteers: Restoration and maintenance work on locomotives and all aspects of railway museum.
Special Skills or Requirements: None but the willingness to work.
Commentary: Everything done at Didcot Restoration and Preservation is done by volunteers. Accommodations on site are limited, but local hotel guest houses can be provided.

Ms. America Goes to Nicaragua

"Are these expeditions safe?" is a frequently asked question about volunteering, particularly about expeditions to isolated wilderness areas or to Third World countries.

Well, that's hard to say. People have different ideas about what is dangerous. Most people who would choose to go on a volunteer vacation wouldn't be frightened by sleeping out in an African jungle, or following wolves across Isle Royale during the night. But many others who would participate in those expeditions would shy away from climbing to the edge of a caldera that was alive with jets of molten lava shooting into the air, or from going into a country divided by civil war.

Betty Meyskens, a self-described Rockwell painting come to life, went to a Third World country as a volunteer, gave little thought to the danger, and not only lived to tell about it, she enjoyed it. A typical American mother of three—"I even used to own a station wagon," she quips—she attended a workshop called "Spirituality of Change," and during one session she said, "I feel a need to roll up my sleeves and dig ditches in Nicaragua."

She thought this was just a statement to indicate how she felt about her life, but several months later she received a calendar of events that listed a Habitat for Humanity project in Nicaragua. On November 19, with little hesitation, she committed herself to going, and she left on February 25. She felt she had to do this, even though she had never considered such an action prior to her impulsive statement at the seminar.

Betty Meyskens and another Habitat for Humanity volunteer tie escribos to rebar to form part of the structural support for a new home in Nicaragua. (Photo courtesy of Betty Meyskens)

"It was all a very mystical experience from the beginning," Meyskens says. "I really didn't know what I was getting myself into. I kept thinking 'Great Adventure' until February 25. Then it was 'Oh, my God! Another fine mess you've got yourself in. I don't know any Spanish. I can't tie rebar.'"

She says it was only then that reality set in. What was she doing going into a country at war? One where only Spanish—which she spoke little of—was spoken, and where you had to bring your own toilet paper if you wanted any.

It was as though Pollyana were going to Nicaragua. Upon her arrival she found that others in the group had made wills before they had left home, while she had given little thought to possible danger. There was little to dispel the others' sense of doom as they passed soldiers, armed with automatic weapons, leaning against lampposts on street corners.

"The war didn't affect us much, though," Meyskens says. "We were stopped at checkpoints as we traveled by flatbed truck along the Pan American Highway to our village, but that was about it. The only signs of the war while we were in the village were the five-man militia stationed there and the occasional helicopter that flew over. Of course many of the families had been affected by death and injury during the long struggles."

Meyskens found some things, such as the presence of soldiers, as she had expected (although still overwhelming), but there were other things that came as pleasant surprises to her. One was the feeling that the people were so materially poor, yet so hopeful and optimistic.

"The 'mañana' stereotype was totally dispelled," she says. Another surprise was the lack of despair, in the village and in herself.

"I didn't feel despair while I was there, although I had certainly expected to," she reports. "The lack of despair and depression on the part of the villagers must have kept it out of my heart.

"I thoroughly enjoyed myself while I was there, and especially liked getting up every morning not having to make any decisions that were so normal at home, such as what to wear. There was only one thing to wear, and you put that on."

She also discovered how she could survive in a difficult situation. Before she had left, she thought about what would be the one thing that would be beyond her ability to cope. Would it be the heat? The fear? The difficult manual labor?

What she found was, at least for this time, none of these was beyond her. In the middle of the trip she asked one of the project coordinators, "Is this it? Is this the hard part?" for she just couldn't believe that she was not only coping, but doing so without difficulty.

Of the experience Meyskens says, "I'll never read a headline or byline from Nicaragua without faces coming up."

After her return from Nicaragua Meyskens wrote the following article for her hometown newspaper as a way of expressing her feelings about her volunteer vacation.

Another Side of Nicaragua

by Betty Meyskens

Ms. America goes to Nicaragua. I guess that is how I saw myself as my Pan Am jet taxied down the runway Saturday night, February 27, headed for Guatemala City and then going on to Managua. I know my going to Nicaragua seemed outlandish to some of my friends. "Don't you know what's going on down there?" Actually I didn't. All I knew was that I wanted to go and see for myself.

I went with 10 other people from Northern California (Mill Valley, Philo, Santa Cruz, and Mendocino). We all went as volunteers with Habitat for Humanity, a nonprofit Christian housing ministry that works in partnership with people in need to provide simple, decent homes.

My construction skills were practically nil, my Spanish elementary, and my knowledge of Central America was

Meyskens and another volunteer pour cement into a mixer in preparation for laying cement blocks for a new home.
(Photo courtesy of Betty Meyskens)

limited to *National Geographic* articles, recent headlines, and hearsay. So although I was eager to go, eager to learn, eager to help, I was also apprehensive. As Pan Am flight 415 lifted off the runway right on schedule, 9:30 P.M., I popped two chloroquine anti-malaria tablets in my mouth.

My adventure had begun.

As the sun rose over the volcanoes, we descended to the Guatemala City Airport. After a short wait and a plane change, we were off to Managua with a short stop in El Salvador. Nine hours after taking off from SFO, we landed at Sandino Airport. Upon deplaning and walking across the tarmac, we all scrambled to focus our cameras and photograph the terminal—our first view of Nicaragua. We were stopped by an airport employee who gently informed us that the airport was considered a military installation, thus no pictures.

We also began to learn the true meaning of the slogan Habitat volunteers live by: "Flexible is not fluid enough." Our luggage had not accompanied us to Managua. Well, it made going through customs simple. All we had were our carry-on bags. Our Habitat coordinators met us in the lobby and ushered us to our transportation, a Toyota flatbed truck.

On the bumpy ride over "Samoza Stone" highway, we asked, "Where is downtown Managua?"

"There is not a downtown Managua," was the reply.

The city was destroyed by an earthquake December 23, 1972. The relief money that poured in was pocketed by Samoza. The revolution gained momentum, and consequently the city was never able to fully rebuild. Shells of buildings stand next to vacant lots. Looking out from the back of the truck I'm in I see the Plaza of the Revolution and the baseball stadium. At a stop light, an oxen-pulled wooden cart is next to me.

The sun is hot at 9:00 A.M.; the air is humid, and the billboard up ahead reads "Radio Sandinista—Audio de la Revolucion."

My three-day stay in Managua consisted of hearing talks by an American-educated Nicaraguan Baptist minister; an

127

engineer for CEPAD (an organization of Protestant churches); the minister of Education; Norman Brent, Mosquito Indian and pastor of the Moravian Church of Managua; and a radio news commentator. My impressions of the country were that there are food, water, electricity, and gasoline shortages. Milk is very hard to find. We were told to fill up with diesel whenever we could find a station that had it, whether we needed it or not.

The lights went out every night in most of Managua about 7:00 P.M. The people seemed to take it in stride and carried on as usual by candlelight. The people we spoke with said that life in Nicaragua is better since the triumph of the Sandinistas, but the revolution is still in progress and there are still problems to be worked through.

Late on the third day we were able to retrieve our luggage and drive along the Pan American Highway to the village of Las Calabazas. The settlement is a dusty little cluster of redbrick square houses with corrugated tin roofs or tile. Skinny dogs, skinny chickens, and skinny pigs meandered through the dirt streets. As our truck bumped and rattled through town, smiling people beamed from their doorways, waving and calling out, "Ola!"

The Habitat housing project sits at the back of the town against the dry hills. I would spend the next two weeks digging trenches for a foundation, moving boulders, tying rebar, shoveling sand, and making cement. Some of us would make roof tiles and mold earth-cement blocks. Our day began at dawn, waking to the sounds of roosters crowing, dogs barking, children chattering, and babies crying. We worked until noon, and then retreated to the shade until two. We worked under the careful guidance of the head contractor, Ramon, a very patient man, and Carlos, our smiling carpenter. We also worked with Flora, Alberto, Juana, and the other future residents of the completed project.

Juana Ruiz is 30 years old. She has six children. Her husband worked on a road repair crew but he was killed in a Contra ambush last year. Juana and her children live in a two-room brick house with her brother and his wife and their children and grandmother. They only have three handmade wooden chairs and a hammock, and a wooden rack on the wall holds plastic plates, bowls, cups, and 15 toothbrushes. Juana and her children will move into one of the Habitat houses when they are complete.

Raina and Teresa are both 22 years old, and they teach preschool in the village. They have 30 students, ages three to five years old, in a very small room with a dirt floor. There are no bright bulletin boards, no Fisher-Price toys, no jungle gyms or teeter totters. In the primary school there are no desks provided, so the children bring desks, carrying them over their heads, from home.

Pencils and paper are shared. The chalkboards are old and scratched, but the arithmetic problems are the same. As I watched the teacher call individual students to work out the problems, I marveled at how hard the teachers work to create order in the midst of chaos, to educate the children against the backdrop of turmoil.

One afternoon I was assigned to Julia, the head ironworker on the housing project. The task seemed simple enough, bend iron rods into square "escribos," to which rebar would be tied to make cement beams. After two hours, I was still fumbling and awkward. I was definitely more trouble than I was worth. But Julia, with all the wonderful patience of Job, and a wonderfully contagious sense of humor, hung in there with me.

I had made 11 perfect escribos! Julia could have made that many in 10 minutes. But she rejoiced with me, hugged and laughed with me, and celebrated my efforts to help. And so that Wednesday afternoon it wasn't that I contributed 11 iron squares that was important. It was that Julia and I formed a bond, a heart connection. We didn't even speak each other's language, but we respected each other, supported each other, and appreciated each other.

Never again will I listen to the news about Nicaragua with the same ear. They are not Communists, Contras, or Sandinistas. They are Julia, Juana, Roman, Carlos, Raina, Teresa, Esmerelda, Jasmina, Alberto, and Eulalia Antonia.

The people of Nicaragua have faces and names. We talked together for 18 days. We hugged together. We sang "La Bamba" together under the stars. We slung picks in the hard, dry earth.

They are not the enemy. The teachers, the bakerwoman, the road crewman, the wood gatherers, the women who grind the corn and make tortillas, the builders, the children— they worked from dawn till dark, and I never once observed any signs of despair. I saw only patience and energy. "Here we surrender never!" is emblazoned everywhere on the walls and waving banners. Perhaps it serves not only as a warning to attacking armies, but also as an affirmation of survival in a country rising to assume its unique place in the world.

As our truck bumped and jostled out of Las Calabazas for the last time, the townspeople followed and waved. Some cried. I cried.

I touched down at SFO Wednesday, March 16, just as the soldiers stationed at Fort Ord were preparing to leave for the Honduran- Nicaraguan border. The country I'd come home to was sending troops to fight the country of my friends I'd just left.

This article originally appeared in the Sebastopol Times & News *of Sebastopol, California.*

Greenpeace, U.S.A.

1436 U St., NW
Washington DC 20009
tel. (202) 462-1177

Project Location: Home office in Washington.
Project Type: Light clerical work.
Project Costs: Volunteers pay all transportation and living costs.
Project Dates: Year-round.
How To Apply: Write to Greenpeace at the above address for information.
Work Done by Volunteers: Light clerical work such as stuffing envelopes, copying, answering and posting mail.
Special Skills or Requirements: Commitment to the Greenpeace cause.
Commentary: While the excitement and headlines of the Greenpeace movement come from the confrontations the organization has with their targeted opponents, none could take place without the volunteers who help raise money and get the word out on what Greenpeace is doing.

Habitat for Humanity

Habitat and Church Sts.
Americus GA 31709
tel. (912) 924-6935

Project Locations: Throughout the U.S. and 30 countries around the world.

Project Type: House building.

Project Costs: Volunteers are responsible for all transportation, room, board, and insurance costs. On overseas workcamps all participants must contribute an amount equal to the cost of one new house, which averages between $1,000 to $3,000. For a group of 10 volunteers, that would mean $100–$300. In U.S. workcamps, costs per participant vary.

Project Dates: U.S. projects generally run for six weeks during the summer, and overseas projects run year-round for two weeks.

How To Apply: Write to Global Village Workcamp Coordinator or Campus Coordinator at the above address for application and information about current projects.

Work Done by Volunteers: General construction.

Special Skills or Requirements: At least one member of each overseas group must speak the language of the host country, and all participants must be at least 18 years old.

Commentary: Habitat is an ecumenical Christian housing ministry that helps build bridges between people as they help those in need build their own houses through "sweat equity."

Sample Projects: In 1990 Habitat had more than 750 participants working in 61 workcamps in 30 countries; 450 students from 32 schools and colleges built houses in Coahoma, Mississippi. The 6-week summer projects will expand to at least 6 locations around the U.S. in 1991.

Heifer Project International
International Livestock Center
Route 2
Perryville AR 72126
tel. (501) 889-5124

Project Locations: Most volunteer positions are at the International Livestock Center, 40 miles west of Little Rock, although there are a few positions in project areas around the world, and others at the regional offices of Heifer Project International.

Project Types: Both individual volunteers and workcamp participants do general ranch work, although some office work is available occasionally for those who find the more difficult ranch work too strenuous.

Project Costs: No registration fee, except for workcamps, which have a $100 fee per group. Individual volunteers who stay for a month or longer receive a small stipend twice a month. Room and board are provided. Volunteers are responsible for preparing their own breakfasts and weekend meals, while all other meals are prepared for the whole group. Volunteer housing, completely furnished, is available. Workcamp volunteers live together in an open-air bunk barn with foam mattresses on wood platforms.

Project Dates: Workcamps are held for one week each during summer months. Other volunteers have no standard length of stay, although most stay six to eight weeks between May and August. Summer staffing for workcamp groups is done with volunteers from late May to late August.

How To Apply: Send to Volunteer Coordinator, Heifer Project International at the above address for brochure and application blank. Specify whether you are interested in applying as an individual, or if you wish to organize a workcamp group.

Work Done by Volunteers: General ranch work. Workcamp groups may spend all week on one project, or they may do a variety of jobs. Other volunteers are given some choice of work according to the needs of the ranch.

Special Skills or Requirements: No ranch or farming skills are necessary, although it is helpful for volunteers who want to work as staff for the workcamps. Workcamp volunteers should be in ninth grade or above for youth camps, and 19 or above for adult camps. Eighteen is the minimum age for general volunteers.

Commentary: Heifer Project International works around the world on projects that help low-income farmers from impoverished areas develop livestock herds (these include cattle, donkeys, sheep, goats, pigs, ducks, rabbits, chickens, and honeybees) by supplying breeding stock and technical know- how, and the International Livestock Center is a 1,225-acre ranch where much of this livestock is held for shipping. There is also a commercial livestock operation at the ranch that helps support the interdenominational activities of the Heifer Project. Much of the money raised for the support of HPI each year comes from the thousands of Sunday school classes across America where young people donate nickels, dimes, and quarters as outreach projects.

Illinois Department of Conservation–Land Management

600 N. Grand Ave. West
Springfield IL 62701- 1787
tel. (217) 782-6752

Project Locations: Statewide in parks.
Project Types: Volunteers in state parks serve as campground hosts, park interpreters, and park technicians.
Project Costs: Volunteers are responsible for all travel and living expenses.
Project Dates: Year-round for varying lengths of time.
How To Apply: Write to the Illinois Department of Conservation–Land Management at the above address for information and application.
Work Done by Volunteers: Campground hosts stay on duty at a state park campground for a minimum of four weeks, working approximately 35 hours per week helping other campers check in and then providing them with needed information about the park. Park interpreters lead educational programs, workshops, hikes, and other activities that enhance visitors' experiences at the parks. They also do some research on the natural vegetation, wildlife, and geology. Park technicians help with the maintenance of the parks and do construction, renovation, and general maintenance work.
Special Skills or Requirements: An interest in parks, a willingness to learn on-the-job, and the ability to follow through are all necessary skills. Campground hosts must be 21 or older.
Commentary: In a period of tight fiscal restraints, volunteers in the parks are as necessary as the paid staff.

Indiana Division of State Parks

616 State Office Bldg.
Indianapolis IN 46204
tel. (317) 232-4124

Project Locations: In parks throughout the state.
Project Types: Landscaping, grounds and trail maintenance.
Project Costs: Entrance fees to parks and camping fees while there.
Project Dates: Year-round.
How To Apply: Contact the above address for a list of parks currently requesting volunteers. Applicants must contact parks directly.
Work Done by Volunteers: Maintenance, gardening, hosting campground, and working in nature centers.
Special Skills or Requirements: Projects are based on the skills of the volunteers, and are selected by park managers.
Commentary: Projects will be developed according to the length of stay. Camping in parks is limited to 14 days, and projects as short as two days can be arranged.
Sample Projects: Campground hosts, trail maintenance and restoration, and landscaping in park.

Interfaith Office on Accompaniment

PO Box 77, Cardinal Station W
Washington DC 20064
tel. (202) 319-5552

Project Location: El Salvador.

Project Type: Accompaniment delegation and long-term volunteers work with and help Salvadoran refugees that are returning to the villages they were forced to leave during the country's long civil war.

Project Costs: Participants are responsible for travel and living costs (approximately $1,100 per trip), and are asked to raise $1,000 in donations in their home community to help support the repopulated villages.

Project Dates: Accompaniment delegate trips were held in June, August, October, November, and December in 1990. Each trip was for 10 days.

How To Apply: Send a letter requesting information to the above address.

Work Done by Volunteers: Education, health care, community and social work, agriculture, computer, reconstruction, etc.

Special Skills or Requirements: Each volunteer is screened for special skills and desire to witness. These villages are frequently in the war zone and all volunteers must recognize the dangers involved.

Commentary: This program has helped more than 10,000 displaced Salvadorans return to their home villages since 1987, and has helped them stay home after they returned.

International Camp Counselor Program/Abroad

356 W. 34th St., 3rd Floor
New York NY 10001
tel. (212) 563-3441

Project Locations: More than 25 countries around the world.

Project Type: Camp counselors.

Project Costs: $100 application fee plus all transportation costs. All camps provide room, board, and insurance, and some also provide a small stipend plus domestic transportation to the camp. The French camps require a week-long course at an additional cost.

Project Dates: All are between June and August except for those in the Southern Hemisphere, which are between December and February. Most require volunteers to stay for the season, although some require only a two-week commitment.

How To Apply: Send to ICCP/Abroad, at the above address, for an application form and brochure. Application deadline for Northern Hemisphere camps is January 1. For Southern Hemisphere, October 1.

Work Done by Volunteers: All positions are for camp counselors, although there is some variety in the type of programs offered by the different camps.

Special Skills or Requirements: Most of the camps have an age requirement of 20 to 30 years of age, and it is desirable to speak the native language. Some camps don't require this, but it helps the volunteers to better understand the culture. Some camps require language fluency. French and Tunisian camps require that the French version of the application forms be completed, for example. Applicants should also have experience working with youth in programs such as scouts, recreational projects, church activities, and schools.

Commentary: This program is operated by the YMCA, and is the counterpart of the inbound International Camp Counselor Program that the YMCA has operated since the early

1950s, which gives young people from around the world an opportunity to come to America to work in camp programs. The abroad program began in the mid-1960s so American youth could have the same opportunity in other countries.

Sample Projects: Below are some sample volunteer positions:

Colombia—two positions, Spanish required for one and helpful for the other. YMCA camp needed a counselor for a general recreation program from mid-June to mid-July, to work with 7- to 14-year-old campers. A private camp with an emphasis in sports needed a counselor from mid-June to mid-August.

Hong Kong—YMCA camp needed one counselor, from late June to mid-August, who could instruct swimming, singing, handicrafts, and games. English or Cantonese was requested. This position paid $30 a week.

Nepal—nonprofit social organization needed one or two volunteers from June to August to run a day camp operation leading sports and academic programs for neighborhood youth. The position included post-camp trekking opportunities for volunteers.

USSR—six to twelve openings for Russian-speaking counselors to work in Soviet Pioneer Camps as co-counselors. This was an exchange program. YMCA camping experience was preferred.

Hungary—up to 20 openings to participate in a program including any or all of the following: summer university sessions, participation in a variety of English-speaking camps, relaxing at Lake Balaton, and sightseeing in Budapest. Hungarian or German helpful.

International Executive Service Corps

PO Box 10005
Stamford CT 06904-2005
tel. (203) 967-6000

Project Locations: Developing countries worldwide, including Eastern Europe.

Project Types: Providing business and technical assistance to a variety of industries and businesses in developing countries.

Project Costs: IESC pays travel and living expenses for volunteer and spouse.

Project Dates: Year-round, with volunteers usually receiving two to three months notice.

How To Apply: Send brief resume to Recruiting Dept., IESC, at the above address.

Work Done by Volunteers: Advisory work, though sometimes hands-on, in various industries. Volunteers sometimes work eight to ten hours per day, six days a week.

Special Skills or Requirements: Industry-specific, hands-on expertise, plus managerial experience. Must be adaptable to different cultures. A foreign language is not essential, but knowledge of French or Spanish is helpful. All volunteers are retired business managers or executives.

Commentary: Projects normally last from two to three months. The word "vacation" applies if working hard and using your experience to help others is a reward for you.

Sample Projects: Establishing a shrimp farm, teaching hand sewing of shoes, establishing a business school, setting up blow-molded plastics manufacturing, computerizing a business enterprise, increasing productivity on a poultry farm, and manufacturing automotive batteries are all recent activities of IESC.

William Waldren: Portrait of the Archaeologist as a Young Artist

by Burkhard Bilger

Bill Waldren has lived the romantic's daydream and found it wanting. In fact, Waldren would do romantics everywhere a favor if he organized a series of lectures at stadiums worldwide. "Being a champion athlete or an important painter or a published poet isn't so hot," he could boom out over loudspeakers to throngs of melancholy adolescents, moon-faced college students, jittery professionals, and wistful homemakers. "I've been all those things and, hey, I got bored. So stop wasting your time with fantasies." Having brought the crowd down, Waldren could then offer an uplifting piece of advice: "If you need a dream," he could say, "imagine being an archaeologist."

Indiana Jones notwithstanding, the idea of spending hours kneeling in the dust searching for bone fragments and worn pottery hardly sets off a Debussy prelude in most people's heads. Yet in 1960, shortly after he stumbled onto a prehistoric burial cave in the hills of Mallorca, Bill Waldren gave up a career as "one of Spain's foremost painters" (according to one Madrid daily), a lucrative gallery contract, and his place in a community of artists—for archaeology. Waldren will assure you that he had all the necessary skills for his new interest—"I learned mapmaking and mechanical drawing during the war, ceramics and sketching in art school, and I taught photography for many years in New York City and

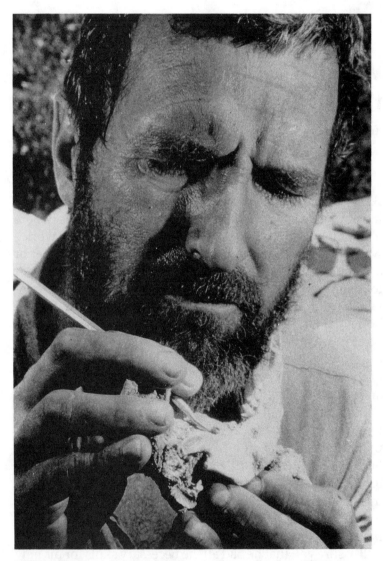

William Waldren demonstrates how to clean a fragile artifact. (Photo courtesy of Earthwatch)

Europe"—but the fact is that he lacked any formal training in archaeology. And he was 36 years old.

Now, in his late sixties, Bill Waldren has rewritten the prehistory of Spain's Balearic Islands. He is the head of a museum, the author of four books on archaeology, a member of the archaeology faculty at Oxford University, and the Winston Churchill Fellow at Cambridge University. When the queen of Spain recently made a trip through Mallorca, she put Waldren's site on her itinerary and agreed to be honorary president of his yearly conference on Spanish prehistory. "I'm the luckiest, happiest man in the world," Waldren tells people with wide-eyed sincerity, "because I do exactly what I want to do." But the grace of his midlife pirouette belies its halting, uncertain beginning and the way in which his old and new lives still intertwine.

"Bill's life story would be perfect for one of those Charles Atlas ads," says Waldren's wife, Jackie. Born two months premature, Waldren weighed only 3½ pounds at birth, and he had rickets. "They had to carry him around on a cushion for the first year of his life," Jackie Waldren says, "and now he's this strapping 180-pound horse."

Waldren still revels in his physicality: shirtless as often as possible and deeply tanned from 15 years of nearly continuous work in the field, he gestures energetically while he talks, stringing together anecdotes with a rolling intensity, often laughing through the words. An opinionated man, Waldren has little patience for either timidity or pretension. Phrases like "there is absolutely no question" and "the proof is completely irrefutable," spoken in a gruff, clipped accent that hints at his New Jersey roots, punctuate his stories. Yet beneath them lies an intellectual flexibility that has defined his life.

The research center in the hill town of Deya, Mallorca, where more than 1,000 Earthwatch volunteers have lived and worked since 1975, was designed and partially built by Waldren. It bears the marks of an artist and an archaeologist: white plaster rooms burrowed like warrens into the hillside, wrought-iron fixtures with a Moorish heaviness, narrow windows slanting sunlight onto a natural rock wall, and heavy brass tea set on the floor. In a corner of the living room lies a scrapbook that provides a fast-forward glimpse of how Waldren arrived at this obscure intellectual and geographic corner of the world. The earliest newspaper clips show a svelte, stern young man roller-skating in 1942, the year Waldren won a national novice figure skating championship (he later toured Europe with Sonja Henie's Holiday on Ice). A few pages later, a faded snapshot shows Bill wearing a trench coat, on leave from the U.S. Army's elite ski patrol. An announcement from 1947 tells of Waldren's first marriage, in St. Patrick's Cathedral, after which he was interviewed on Walter Winchell's radio show, "Breakfast with the New-lyweds." Finally, photographs from the early 1950s show Waldren, the "first Existentialist painter in Paris" (by his own reckoning), wearing a black turtleneck, slumped onto one elbow, pinching a cigarette between thumb and forefinger, aloof to the canvases splattered with rough white plaster behind him.

It's an impressive sequence, and the photos are strangely seductive: the man in each picture conforms comfortably to his role, as if he were living exactly the life we imagine athletes, soldiers, or painters to live. Yet one look at a picture of Bill Waldren today—perched, with a broad, easy grin, on a pile of rocks and wielding a pickax—destroys the illusion of the earlier photographs. Looking nothing like a "real" archaeologist, Waldren today makes you wonder why archaeologists don't all look like him.

By the time Waldren arrived in Mallorca from France, in 1953, painting had already lost some of its allure for him. "The art scene in Paris finally went sour for me—gallery directors, the critics, everyone who runs art even though they know nothing about it," he says. The town of Deya seemed an ideal retreat: painters, sculptors who worked with exquisitely tortured olive wood, and poets (among them Robert Graves) haunted its winding cobbled streets by day and its terraced cafes by night. At first, Waldren fit into the scene inconspicuously, giving regular shows of his paintings and solidifying his reputation in Spanish and American circles. The fluid, abstract style of his paintings from that period is still evident in the silver jewelry that Waldren makes. "I don't like to will the silver into any shape," he explains. "I just wait until the molten metal assumes a shape that I find interesting or beautiful, and then I freeze it in that position." But while he sold paintings to major galleries on the East and West Coasts, the drinking and smoking that accompanied the art scene gradually wore him down. "It was all part of the image at the time," he admits. "I thought it brought charisma."

Financially, Waldren's art career continued to improve until, in 1960, he landed a year-round contract with the prestigious Dwan Gallery in Los Angeles. It was then that he made his first archaeological discovery. "I was walking across the countryside one morning to get some relief from painting," he recalls, "when I passed this perfect little cave in the side of a hill." Even before Waldren looked inside and found a pyramid of Copper Age skulls and piles of leg bones, the cave opening amplified a chord that had been ringing inside him for some time. "There is no better place to look at the world than from the mouth of a cave," he explains, "It's like staring into a fire: it stirs something primordial in you. . . ."

He began digging almost immediately, discovering a nearby rock shelter and, two years later, a second cave at Son Muleta. In 1964, Waldren severed his contract with the Dwan Gallery. "Once I realized that it wasn't the art itself, but having a medium through which to channel all your creativity that mattered, all the rest followed," he says.

Son Muleta was Waldren's proving ground, and he excavated it with an ambition and obsessive care that have characterized his work ever since. In order to haul every grain of earth up and out of the cave, he devised a system of pulleys and buckets that threaded through it. "We set up a system of seven gradually finer screens to sort through all the earth. The last one was as dense as a carburetor filter." Any remains were cleaned with water piped from an obliging neighbors's swimming pool, 400 yards away, and meticulously documented. "By the time we got to the finest screens," Waldren remembers, "we were finding lizard jaws, tiny ear bones, and vertebrae half the size of the head of a pin." As they approached the darkest, deepest levels of the cave, he could only afford to excavate by candlelight.

Waldren now devoted himself entirely to archaeology— although he decorated a discotheque or two in Palma for spare cash along the way. But 13 years passed before he resolved to apply to Oxford's archaeology program. "I was scared," he says. "I was 50 years old; I didn't need any disappointments at that point in my life." After several grueling interviews with ever-larger boards of distinguished Oxford dons, he was finally accepted into Linacre College in 1975. That same year Waldren received his first grant from Earthwatch, to excavate a Copper Age rock shelter at Son Matge.

"It was something of a gamble," remembers Betsy Caney, then head of the Center for Field Research. "Earthwatch was just getting its legs as a viable, respectable source of funding, and we really wanted researchers with doctorates. But Waldren seemed to be onto something." Indeed, Waldren's obsessive work at Son Muleta was rewarded. By the time his crews stopped digging, they had tunneled 10 feet into the hillside and 34 feet down ("I can still smell the candles burning down there," Waldren says), uncovering dozens of primitive antelope skeletons and the oldest human remains ever found in the Balearic Islands.

Still, Waldren had never been to college, and the sudden immersion into academia was exhausting at first. "He had to do a lot of rewriting in the beginning," Jackie Waldren remembers, "and he wanted to get so many years of research into that thesis." The product of eight years' labor, Waldren's four-volume doctoral work now sits like a miniature Stonehenge on his mantelpiece. In it he was able to draw the first hypotheses about Mallorca's primitive ecology and the state of its Copper Age culture. Later sites would help him illuminate Mallorca's early pottery styles, its nascent contact and trade with other Mediterranean cultures, and its earliest

146

religious cults, as well as establish a full chronology of the Mallorcan Copper Age, beginning around 2500 B.C. Because events on the Balearic Islands paralleled those on the mainland, Waldren's work helped clarify economic changes throughout the Copper Age Mediterranean. "I imagine that lots of academics sniffed at him at first." Peter Tead, a publisher and long-time friend of Waldren's says, "but his results have made them stop. It's reassuring that a man like Bill can still climb the ladder in his way."

Waldren is particularly proud of the part that volunteers have played in his achievements. The Deya Research Center itself is designed to incorporate them into his life: dormitory rooms with bunks and cozy rounded ceilings lie adjacent to darkrooms and laboratories. The Waldrens' veranda can easily accommodate 30 diggers listening, in the languorous evening air, to Waldren's stories of Robert Graves and Mallorca before tourism, or his wife's analyses of Mallorcan society (she recently earned a Ph.D. in anthropology at Oxford).

Because he was for so long an uncredentialed archaeology enthusiast, Waldren has always had a special touch with volunteers. "I defy anyone to be so awkward or cumbersome that they can't do this," he will tell a group of new volunteers in a mock bullying tone, while demonstrating how to determine the shape of a bowl from a solitary shard. Later, lecturing on Mallorca's early pottery styles, he will infuse the same humble chunk of pottery with human history: "This wasn't poured into a mold and put out by the thousands," he'll explain. "Somebody had his hands all over this; he put it into the fire; he might have stopped and said, 'Hey, I like the shape of that.' It has significance." Often, Waldren has his teams shape pots of their own and bake them in outdoor kilns to further bring prehistoric Mallorcan crafts to life.

Many volunteers come to Mallorca, as Waldren himself probably did, for the weather, the exotic landscape, and the cosmopolitan flavor. But time spent at the site, overseen by the man's consuming, restless energy, has inspired at least 3 volunteers in the last 17 years to become archaeologists. One of them, an English professor at Columbia University when he first arrived in Mallorca, went on to get his masters degree from Oxford and now teaches archaeology in Florida. Another, a former air force man retired from the Strategic Air Command, now teaches archaeology at the University of North Dakota. The third, a grandmother and former interior designer, has been accepted into Oxford's doctoral program in archaeology. For each of them, as for Waldren 30 years ago, a stay on the island was enough to freeze the fluid stuff of their lives, like molten silver, into a strange but fascinating shape.

This article was originally published in Earthwatch, *the quarterly bulletin of Earthwatch.*

International Expeditions, Inc.

1776 Independence Ct., Suite 104
Birmingham AL 35216
tel. (205) 870-5550

Commentary: International Expeditions has two programs,
Zoo and Aquarium Travel Association and the International
Program for Scholarly Exchange, which are similar to the
programs run by Earthwatch and the Foundation for Field
Research; scholars apply to them for funding of research
projects, and interested travelers are then assessed a fee for
participating in the project. They are, however, different in
several ways.

First, International Expeditions offers scholars two choices
as to how the travelers will participate in the research
project—as active participants, very much like Earthwatch
projects, or as passive participants. With this second choice,
the travelers who have helped fund the research project are
involved in visiting the site on a guided tour, watching the
research activities, and sitting in on some lectures about the
project. They do not actively participate as volunteer
workers, however.

Second, International Expeditions is a travel agency that
arranges all the tours to research project sites, in addition to
other guided tours that observe the natural wonders of the
world. International Expeditions is much more for those
people who want to support scientific research and watch
the scientists in action, than for those interested in getting
down on their hands and knees to collect data.

International Eye Foundation

7801 Norfolk Ave.
Bethesda MD 20814
tel. (301) 986-1830

Project Locations: Throughout the Third World.
Project Types: Prevention and care of blindness and primary eye care training of indigenous health workers.
Project Costs: Vary.
Project Dates: Throughout the year.
How To Apply: Send to the International Eye Foundation at the above address for brochure and application form.
Work Done by Volunteers: Primarily training nurses, paramedical personnel, village health workers, and others to give primary eye care to local populations. Training of professional ophthalmologists, ophthalmic nurses, and ophthalmic technicians is also a major service offered by IEF.
Special Skills or Requirements: All volunteers must be ophthalmologists, certified ophthalmic technologists or technicians, or ophthalmic nurses.
Commentary: Of the 42 million blind in the world, 4 out of 5 have conditions that are preventable or curable, and in the Third World there is often only one ophthalmologist for every 5 million people. IEF attempts to alleviate this problem by training local populations to work in eye care, and since more than half of the visual defects in the world can be treated by health workers as well as by doctors, their work does much to solve the problem.

International Fourth World Movement

7600 Willow Hill Dr.
Landover MD 20785
tel. (301) 336-9489

Project Locations: Workcamps in Washington, DC area, France, and other European countries. Internships in New York and Washington.

Project Types: Two-week summer workcamps and two-month internships for those exploring long-term commitments to fighting poverty.

Project Costs: Contribution to cost of food, plus transportation.

Project Dates: Internships can be anytime during the year. Workcamps are for two weeks during the summer.

How To Apply: For more information and application form, send a stamped, self-addressed envelope to International Fourth World Movement at the above address, with a letter including your comments and personal observations about extreme poverty.

Work Done by Volunteers: Interns do work that is determined by their skills and the needs of the national office at the time of selection. Volunteers in workcamps do manual labor and office work at the movement's centers. They also view videos and participate in discussions about the effects of extreme poverty.

Special Skills or Requirements: A willingness to learn from the poorest families around the world.

Commentary: In both industrialized and developing countries, some families are so poor that they are left out of their society's progress. The Fourth World Movement is an expression of these people's will to participate.

Sample Projects: Street libraries—with books, computers, and art materials, the movement's long-term volunteers seek out the poorest children in urban shelters, welfare hotels, and isolated mountain villages. By coming to their neighborhoods, the volunteers can enable parents to get involved in their children's futures.

International Research Expeditions

140 University Dr.
Menlo Park CA 94025
tel. (415) 323-4228

Project Locations: Throughout the world.
Project Types: Scientific research projects in archaeology, biology, animal behavior, entomology, ornithology, botany, zoology, and marine biology.
Project Costs: From $400 to $1,800, plus transportation to site.
Project Dates: Year- round.
How To Apply: Send to the above for application and brochure.
Work Done by Volunteers: Assist with a variety of scientific research projects.
Special Skills or Requirements: Some projects require special skills such as scuba certification or canoeing, but most only require an interest in the project and the ability to follow instructions.
Commentary: This is another nonprofit organization that works with university scientists and helps them find both funding and volunteers to further their research.

Interplast, Inc.

2458 Embarcadero Way
Palo Alto CA 94303
tel. (415) 424-0123

Project Locations: Mexico, Honduras, Peru, Brazil, Ecuador, Nepal, Western Samoa, Jamaica, Bolivia, Vietnam, Bangladesh, and Dominican Republic.

Project Type: Reconstructive surgery in underdeveloped countries.

Project Costs: Vary by project.

Project Dates: Most projects are in fall, winter, and spring.

How To Apply: Send to Marge Sentous, Interplast, Inc., at the above address for application form and information.

Work Done by Volunteers: Medical work on reconstructive surgery.

Special Skills or Requirements: All volunteers must be plastic surgeons, anesthesiologists, pediatricians, operating room nurses, or recovery room nurses.

Commentary: Another medical volunteer organization that offers free help to Third World countries that they otherwise would not receive.

Intersea Research

PO Box 1667
Friday Harbor WA 98250
tel. (206) 378-5980

Project Locations: Aboard the 126-foot classic fantail yacht *Acania* in southeast Alaska during the summer, and the South Pacific in the winter.

Project Type: Whale research.

Project Costs: $2,490 for the 11-day Alaskan trips. This covers all meals and accommodations from noon on the first day of program to noon of the last day. It does not include laundry and other personal expenses, or meals ashore.

Project Dates: Early June to late September for the northern trips, and midwinter for the Pacific ones.

How To Apply: Send to Intersea Research at the above address for more information and application forms.

Work Done by Volunteers: The primary work done by volunteers is collecting evidence on the feeding behavior of the humpback whale and photographing tail flukes for use in identifying individual whales. Acoustical recordings are also made when feasible.

Special Skills or Requirements: The requirements are minimal. Anyone over 14 may participate, although volunteers who have skills in photography or animal identification are likely to be given priority on trips that are in high demand.

Commentary: This program is similar to that operated by the Cousteau Society, but is much more intimate.

Involvement Corps

15515 Sunset Blvd., Suite 108
Pacific Palisades CA 90272
tel. (213) 459-1022

The Involvement Corps is a special organization that serves as a link between volunteers from the nation's work force and the communities in which they live. It assists both corporations and local agencies in carrying out programs that meet their needs. The organization designs community involvement programs and projects and works directly with senior management of corporations in order to help them become involved with their local communities.

The Involvement Corps was founded in 1968, and has worked with more than 150 companies in 13 states and the District of Columbia. One of these is Transamerica Occidental Life in Los Angeles, where in one recent year more than 1,200 of the company's 4,000 employees volunteered more than 6,500 hours in 20 community agencies affiliated with Involvement Corps.

Have your company get involved with Involvement Corps and get involved in your community.

Involvement Volunteers

PO Box 218
Port Melbourne, Victoria, Australia, 3207
tel. International 61-3-646-5504

Project Locations: Australia, Fiji, and India.

Project Types: Urban or rural revegetation, seed collection, propagation, planting, and maintenance; marine archaeology; historic building restoration; working in gardens, parks, and museums; bird observatory operations; and assisting with sport and education organizations for the disadvantaged.

Project Costs: In 1990 the costs were AU $300, plus travel costs to work sites. Room and board can range from nothing to AU $78 per week.

Project Dates: Throughout the year.

How To Apply: Send for application and information sheet to the above address, or to Involvement Corps, Inc., 15515 Sunset Blvd., #108, Pacific Palisades, CA 90272; tel. (213) 459-1022.

Work Done by Volunteers: Most work is labor-intensive, but in a wide variety of efforts.

Special Skills or Requirements: All volunteers must understand spoken English, and any special skills will be utilized on each project as possible.

Commentary: Involvement Volunteers began as a locally developed project to get volunteers involved in saving the environment, and has grown into a national and international program that helps volunteers participate in a wide range of community-based, not-for-profit organizations. Many, but not all, of these relate to the conservation of the environment.

To assist volunteers from overseas, Involvement Volunteers has developed a package that includes information on:

1. seeking and negotiating suitable volunteer placements;
2. applying for a visa;

3. meeting volunteers at the Melbourne airport and providing their first night's accommodations;

4. the Australian banking and taxation system;

5. a communications base and redirecting mail to volunteers;

6. paid fruit-picking positions to help them supplement their funds;

7. the purchase of discounted Australia coachline tickets and PADI scuba open-water diving courses;

8. and additional support and advice where and when necessary to make visitors' time in Australia as beneficial and comfortable as possible for all concerned.

French Restorations

Chantiers is a French word that embodies the idea of cooperation to achieve a common goal. This idea, for at least the past quarter century, has included the use of volunteers as an important part of the restoration of medieval villages, castles, and churches in France. The number of both French and American volunteer organizations involving the *chantiers* concept of cooperation is increasing rapidly, and they annually recruit hundreds of workers who spend from two weeks to a whole summer working on restoration projects.

After her summer in France, Cindy Corlett, a student at the College of William and Mary in Williamsburg, Virginia, wrote the following article.

Excavation in Faverges

by Cindy Corlett

Lately I have been dreaming about opening my bedroom door and stepping out onto a balcony overlooking the French Alps. There would be no urban cacophony, no dorm-life clutter. I would see only strawberry gardens below, and snow-covered mountains beyond. The sunsets would be beautiful, red and yellow streaks lingering after the azure hues slip behind Mt. L'Arclosan.

My dream is in fact a vivid memory. I spent many evenings on these balconies when I was "home" at my boarding school residences in Faverges, France last summer. I lived there for a month as a volunteer on an archaeological excavation organized by Renaissance du Chateau.

158

Volunteers excavate the Gallo-Roman villa Le Thovey in Faverges, France. (Photo courtesy of Robert F. Jeantet)

I was one of 16 North Americans on the dig. We were a varied group, including a retired fireman, an accountant, and students from several colleges. Together, we concentrated on the excavation of a Gallo-Roman bath and villa called Le Thovey.

Some participants were experienced archaeologists; others were first-time diggers like myself. We made steady progress, uncovering columns, walls, floors, pottery, and metal objects. At the end of the month, the mayor rewarded us with personal thanks and a reception at the town hall.

Le Thovey has been undergoing excavation since its discovery in 1981. The site directors, Michel Duret and Alain Piccamiglio, date the complex from the first century B.C. to A.D. 270 Foundations and floor comprise the majority of the

159

remains. The dig is shallow, the significant strata lying within approximately three meters of the surface. One complete Tuscan column and two partial ones have been reerected above ground; the sight of them attracts many tourists.

Much of our work last summer focused on the baths. After striking the bottom of the cauldarium (hot bath), I found its floor and most of its walls intact, complete with pink mortar linings. One group member discovered a lead pipe that was part of the underground water transport system.

The archaeologists freely provided historical information and shared their regional culture. I learned that centuries ago the stream that fed the baths was believed to have healing properties and spiritual significance. (The site was a shrine in ancient times.) Older locals of Haute-Savoy still believe in the water's power to improve vision.

Our days were structured around work at Le Thovey, but they incorporated much more. Mornings began with fresh baguettes and bowls of coffee. We took turns running to the boulangerie (bakery) to shop. Bicycles were provided for us to ride from the boarding school to the site. After working from eight to eleven, we ate lunch at one of Faverges' best restaurants. The four-course meals were cultural studies in themselves. Afternoons were free to spend as we wished. Later in the day we dug for another hour and a half, showered, relaxed on the balconies, and prepared and ate supper. Trips to cafes and locals' homes provided evening entertainment.

Weekend and Wednesday trips were part of the program. French friends invited some of us hiking and mountain-climbing. Hang-gliding (via deltaplanes) was an activity option. All of the activities were optional, but transportation was always provided. Four of us from the program rented a hotel room on the Ile de la Cite in Paris after leaving Faverges. Seeing the city was a perfect complement to the program.

This article was originally published in the March 1988 issue of Transitions Abroad.

Ironbridge Gorge Museum Trust

The Wharfage, Ironbridge
Telford, Shropshire TF8 7AW, England
tel. Ironbridge (095245) 3522

Project Location: Shropshire, England, three hours from London.

Project Type: Some volunteers staff working exhibits, while others are involved in archaeology, research, cataloging, engineering, and conservation.

Project Costs: The museum has constructed volunteer dormitories with bunk beds, fully equipped kitchens, and laundry facilities. To help cover their operating costs, a small nightly fee is charged for using the dorms. The museum has insurance to cover all volunteers, but volunteers are responsible for all transportation and food costs.

Project Dates: Volunteers are accepted from February to October for varying stays.

How To Apply: Write to Lawrence Knott, Volunteer Organizer, Ironbridge Gorge Museum Trust, at the above address for information and an application form.

Work Done by Volunteers: A wide variety, with volunteers asked to state their preference upon application. The museum makes every attempt to meet the wishes of the volunteers, but may have to assign them to other tasks as the need arises. Volunteers are expected to spend the majority of their time working for the museum, but a flexible approach is taken on scheduling work hours so volunteers can visit other parts of the area.

Special Skills or Requirements: No special requirements are stated, but volunteers are expected to be willing to work hard, and to have a flexible approach to life.

Commentary: Shropshire was the cradle of the Industrial Revolution, and Ironbridge was named after the first iron bridge to be built in the world, which was constructed over the River Severn in 1779. The process of using coke instead of charcoal to smelt iron instead of charcoal was perfected in

Coalbrookdale in 1709, and many other firsts have occurred in the region. The first iron boat and first iron aqueduct were also built there, and in 1802, Richard Trevithick built the first steam locomotive there.

The Ironbridge Museum Trust was established in 1971, and the museum has grown so in size and reputation that it now draws more than 250,000 visitors each year. There have been many links between the Ironbridge area and America in the past 200 years, and Americans are very welcome as volunteers in the museum.

Joint Assistance Centre

H-65, South Extn.-1
New Delhi, 110 049, India

Project Locations: Most volunteers work in New Delhi, but there are a number of projects around the country.

Project Type: Work in New Delhi is generally office work, but other projects involve manual labor and study.

Project Costs: Volunteers are responsible for all transportation to project site, as well as insurance costs, a registration fee of $20, and a monthly contribution of approximately $100. No visitors to India may receive any remuneration for work or study, and volunteers who do work must make a contribution to the organization that is sponsoring them, and apply for a tourist visa only.

Project Dates: Volunteers may come at any time during the year, although workcamps are at specific times. Their dates are generally set by December of previous year.

How To Apply: Send to Convener, Joint Assistance Centre, at the above address, with three international postal reply coupons for information and application.

Work Done by Volunteers: Varies from general office, to fundraising, to general construction, to editing and helping in exhibitions and seminars.

Special Skills or Requirements: Journalism, library, typing, and stenography are all special skills that are needed in the offices. General construction skills and accommodating nature are needed in the workcamps.

Commentary: JAC is a voluntary, nongovernmental organization that is attempting to improve the disaster preparedness of the people of India. Volunteers must be able to function in a culture very different from that of the West. In the workcamps there are very stringent rules concerning living conditions and activities. Only vegetarian food is served, with no smoking, drugs, or alcohol allowed, and living quarters are primitive. JAC is also involved in alternative, nontraditional medicine and offers volunteers homeopathy and solar therapy, although volunteers may consult other doctors for any illness they have while in a camp. This program is an excellent way for Americans to gain firsthand knowledge of India and its culture.

Kansas Archaeology Training Program

Kansas State Historical Society
120 W. 10th St.
Topeka KS 66612
tel. (913) 296-4779

Project Locations: All projects are within Kansas.
Project Types: Archaeological excavations of prehistoric and historic sites.
Project Costs: Participants must join the Kansas Anthropological Association ($12 per year), and pay all transportation, room, and board. Motels and camping are always available near the project sites.
Project Dates: First two weeks of June each year.
How To Apply: Send a letter of interest to the above address.
Work Done by Volunteers: Archaeological excavation and laboratory work, specialized processing of artifacts, and/or formal class instruction.
Special Skills or Requirements: Volunteers must be at least 10 years of age. Those between the ages of 10 and 14 must work with a sponsoring adult.
Commentary: The Kansas Archaeology Training Program is a cooperative effort of the Kansas State Historical Society and the Kansas Anthropological Association. It began in 1975 and offers volunteers the opportunity to participate in the scientific excavation of important archaeological sites. The program is structured as an educational experience in which participants may be involved in a wide range of excavation and laboratory functions.
Sample Projects: Past projects have included work on a wide range of prehistoric and historic sites in all parts of the state.

Kenya Voluntary Development Association

PO Box 48902
Nairobi, Kenya
tel. 25379

Project Location: Rural areas of Kenya.
Project Type: Community development projects.
Project Costs: About $200.
Project Dates: Two-week projects held in March/April, July/August, and November/December each year.
How To Apply: Write to Director at the above address at least four months in advance of the projects you are interested in.
Work Done by Volunteers: Volunteers work with members of the local communities, under the supervision of local experts and instructors.
Special Skills or Requirements: No special skills, except ability to live in a new culture, are required.
Commentary: KVDA is an indigenously inspired and oriented organization that each year offers youth and adults, from Africa and overseas, opportunities to serve in Kenya's rural and/or needy areas during their free time and holidays.
Sample Projects: Past projects have helped construct dams, bridges, health centers, homes for teachers, and similar public development projects.

Koinonia Partners

Route 2
Americus GA 31709-9986
tel. (912) 924-0391

Project Location: Americus, Georgia.
Project Types: Farm, production, construction, and office work.
Project Costs: None. Volunteers receive a small stipend.
Project Dates: Sessions are normally March through May, June through August, September through December, with a special short session in January. Some volunteers stay longer.
How To Apply: Send to Gail Steiner, Volunteer Program, Koinonia Partners, at the above address, for program information and application form.
Work Done by Volunteers: Koinonia builds houses for the poor, operates a working farm, and processes food products for mail order, and runs youth programs in local neighborhoods. All volunteers join with Koinonia partners in all the work on the farm. From 8:00 A.M. until 5:00 P.M. each day all volunteers work on demanding jobs that are often repetitious.
Special Skills or Requirements: Although volunteers need not be Christians, Koinonia states that they "unashamedly study the teaching of Jesus." The partners practice a radical discipleship in the use of their time and environment, and spend much time discussing theological differences, which volunteers are expected to participate in.
Commentary: Koinonia Farms, the predecessor of Koinonia Partners, was started as an experiment in Christian living in 1942 by Clarence and Florence Jordan and Martin and Mabel England. They had two goals: to live in the community and bear Christian witness, and to help local farmers improve their techniques. Koinonia faced increasing hostility in the 1950s, however, because of its position against racial prejudice. By 1968 only two families remained at the farm, and it seemed destined to close. In 1969, through the efforts of many, Koinonia Farms became Koinonia Partners and

gained new life. A prominent part of this new program was to bring volunteers in groups of eight to ten, of all ages, to Koinonia for three months in a work-study program. This is still an integral part of Koinonia Partners, and continues to bring new ideas to them.

La Sabranenque Restoration Projects

in France:
Saint Victor la Coste
30290 Laudun, France
tel. (33) 66 50 05 05

in U.S.:
c/o Simon
217 High Park Blvd.
Buffalo NY 14226
tel. (716) 836-8698

Project Locations: Several sites in southern France in Saint Victor la Coste, near Avignon, and three sites in Italy. One in Gnallo, a small hamlet in northern Italy, one in Settefonti, near Bologna in central Italy, and one in Montescaglioso in the south.

Project Types: Restoration of simple monuments, small structures, villages, and sites that are typical of the traditional regional architecture (medieval chapels, old village buildings, and other structures that are property of villages and nonprofit organizations).

Project Costs: $710 for three-week project, half in France, half in Italy. $380 for a two-week project in France.

Project Dates: Two- and three-week periods throughout June, July, and August.

How To Apply: Send to one of the above addresses for more information and applications.

Work Done by Volunteers: Volunteers participate directly in restoration projects, learning building skills on-the-job and becoming part of an international team. Specific projects will depend upon time of arrival, since all projects are ongoing.

Special Skills or Requirements: No previous experience necessary (very few volunteers have any previous building experience), and project organizers speak French, English, and Italian.

Commentary: Projects offer participants the opportunity to enter into the life of Mediterranean villages while taking an active part in practical, cooperative, and creative projects. Volunteers live in houses in Saint Victor la Coste, or in a house at Italian sites.

Sample Projects: Projects are aimed at the preservation, restoration, reconstruction, and revitalization of rural sites, and for the preservation of the rural habitat. Techniques learned and used by volunteers include stonemasonry, stone cutting, simple carpentry, floor and roof tiling, etc. In 1987, volunteers did a complete roof reconstruction, restored walls, buttresses, and window openings, and constructed a small stairway at the medieval chapel of Gaujac, 10 miles from St. Victor la Coste.

Lesotho Workcamps Association

PO Box 6
Maseru—100
Lesotho, South Africa
tel. (050) 314862

Project Locations: Various villages throughout Lesotho.
Project Type: Workcamps.
Project Costs: $75 registration fee.
Project Dates: June, July, December, and January.
How To Apply: Contact the above address or apply through one of the partner organizations in the U.S.
Work Done by Volunteers: Primarily construction, with some forestation and soil conservation projects.
Special Skills or Requirements: Lesotho prefers volunteers to have previous workcamp experience, or basic skills in projects being undertaken.
Commentary: Operation Crossroads Africa is one of the North American partner organizations.
Sample Projects: These workcamps are composed of 20 volunteers per project, working for three weeks with local residents building classrooms, digging pit latrines, improving water supplies, and planting forests.

Ironbridge Gorge and an Unusual Train Tour of Great Britain

In 1709 Abraham Darby perfected the technique of smelting iron ore with coke instead of charcoal, giving birth to the Industrial Revolution.

In the century that followed, many other firsts occurred in the valley of the River Severn. The first iron bridge, iron boat, and iron aqueduct were all built in the factories of the region, and in 1802 the first steam locomotive rolled out of a factory in Coalbrookdale.

This valley is steeped in history: the history of a revolution that continues, the history of ideas as well as action. The action continues to this day, but now it involves reconstruction and restoration, rather than construction.

Buildings and factories stand as monuments to that pioneering period, restored by workers of the Ironbridge Gorge Museum Trust, which was founded in 1967 to preserve and interpret the life of Coalbrookdale and Ironbridge at the birth of the Industrial Revolution.

The memories of furnaces that roared to life and brought dramatic changes to Western Civilization, and ultimately the whole world, as well as to the restored buildings that housed their adjoining factories, today bring over a quarter of a million visitors a year to Ironbridge Gorge. These visitors appreciate the volunteer labor that has played such a large role in the development of the museum. The restored buildings and the exhibits in them wouldn't exist without the

172

thousands of hours donated by volunteers from Great Britain and abroad. And many more hours are donated each year to help increase the scope of existing exhibits, build new ones, and restore more artifacts.

While Ironbridge is a British museum staffed primarily by residents of the British Isles, volunteers are accepted from around the world. And Americans who visit or volunteer at the museum will find many links with their own past.

Ironbridge was begun in 1776, the year the American Revolution began, and the Darby family included many members who were prominent Quakers with many associates in America.

In addition, the first monument outside the U.S. to be honored by the American Society of Civil Engineers as a "Civil Engineering Landmark" was the Iron Bridge.

There are ample opportunities for volunteers at Ironbridge Gorge, and great flexibility. A tour as volunteer here adds immeasurably to one's knowledge of one of the most important revolutions of all times.

But such a stay might be only the beginning of a volunteer tour of Great Britain. One of the greatest achievements of the

A gang of track-laying volunteers rests during a job in County Antrium, Ireland. (Photo courtesy of Bill McMillon)

Industrial Revolution was the development of Great Britain's extensive rail system, and many of those early railways are still in operation, run mostly by volunteer organizations.

The lure of the sites, sounds, and smells of steam locomotives is even greater to many people than the development of the industrial techniques that made the construction of these amazing vehicles possible.

For those of you who are drawn to steam railroads, there are dozens throughout Great Britain that not only welcome volunteers, but couldn't function without them. One of these is the Ffestiniog Railway of Wales. The Ffestiniog is the busiest independent railway in Great Britain and is operated by the oldest continuously operating railway company in the world. And, although it's not a museum, it abounds in industrial archaeology with rolling stock that goes back over 100 years to the early days of railroads.

Volunteers work in signals and telecommunications, in the railway museum, in the maintenance shop, and on the rails.

If you are a railroad buff you can have your grandest dreams come true on the Ffestiniog and other working railways of Great Britain as you take a most unusual rail tour of the British Isles. From the Ffestiniog, which began as a mining railway in northern Wales, a rail tour of Great Britain can take you to Northern Ireland, Scotland, North Yorkshire, Oxfordshire, Devon, and Dorset. All as a working member of a rail crew on some of the oldest railways in the world.

The Railway Preservation Society of Ireland operates rail tours throughout Ireland, primarily in the North, and uses volunteers on a variety of projects year-round. From Londonderry to Belfast to Dublin, this part of the rail tour gives you an opportunity to see Ireland, and to help restore some of its industrial heritage.

From Ireland you can continue to Scotland where the Lochty Private Railway is located. It runs in farm country to the south of St. Andrews in one of the most scenic areas of Scotland, and was a goods line that ran to a small farming community in Fife between 1898 and 1966, when not only was service discontinued, but the track was lifted.

Later that year John Cameron bought the farm through which the last mile of track had run. He had always been interested in railroads and soon began reconstruction of the track to accommodate a locomotive he had acquired.

This was the beginning of the Lochty Private Railway, which today makes extensive use of volunteer labor.

Just below the North Yorkshire Moors National Park along the northeast coast of England is the North Yorkshire Moors Railway. Beginning in Pickering, this 18-mile railway prefers volunteers between March and September, when major projects are undertaken.

Your rail tour continues to Oxfordshire, where, in 1961, a group of students organized to help preserve a typical Great Western Railway branch line steam train, and marked the beginning of the Great Western Society. Today this society operates a working museum and railway in Didcot, which is about 50 miles west of London and 10 miles south of Oxford.

To the west of Didcot, in Gloucestershire, is the Royal Forest of Dean. This area was declared a royal hunting forest by King Canute in 1016. Despite a checkered history, the forest is still in the hands of the Crown, and though the area is one of great natural beauty, it is also an industrial area. Another of England's historic steam railways, the Dean Forest Railway, is found in the forest.

This railway was the Lydney Junction–Parkend branch line until British Rail announced its closure in 1970, when a group of dedicated steam enthusiasts quickly mounted a campaign to reopen the line. They called themselves the Dean Forest Railway Society, and today operate a four-mile line with restored stock.

From the Forest of Dean the rail tour continues south to Devon, where the Dart Valley Railway Association operates two lengths of track, one just outside the Dartmoor National Park, and the other near the coast of the English Channel.

These are only a few of the steam railways of Great Britain that you can visit and work on. Many of them are located in heavy industrial areas, but others, such as those mentioned here, are located in beautiful natural settings that give you, as a volunteer and railroad buff, an opportunity to visit historical as well as natural sites of Great Britain, while having the experience of a lifetime: unlimited opportunity to work on and around steam trains.

Lisle Fellowship, Inc.

433 W. Sterns Rd.
Temperance MI 48182
tel. (313) 847-7126

Project Locations: Can be at a number of sites in the world. In 1990 they had programs in India, Bali, Ohio, and South Dakota.

Project Types: These aren't traditional projects. Lisle has attempted to integrate human relations in multicultural groups with field experience. One project, which has been held in Toledo, Ohio since 1987, is a one-week Elderhostel program.

Project Costs: Costs vary tremendously by project, but are kept to a minimum.

Project Dates: All projects are in the summer, and vary in length. The India project was six weeks; the Bali and South Dakota projects, three weeks.

How To Apply: Send to Lisle Fellowship at the above address for information and application forms.

Work Done by Volunteers: Volunteers spend their time in a variety of activities on Lisle projects. Cultural discussions, opportunities to experience the cultural activities introduced in the discussions, and working side-by-side with local residents on subsistence projects, and sharing about the effects of these experiences for the individuals involved, are only a few of the experiences Lisle attempts to give volunteers.

Special Skills or Requirements: Participants are generally over 18, and the normal age range is from 18 to 75. All applicants are asked to consider the special demands of the Lisle format, which requires the ability to live in a cooperative, group-living situation with a consensual decision- making process, with the added responsibility of doing so in an intercultural group.

Commentary: The Lisle Fellowship is different from many organizations in this guide. While productive work is one goal of the fellowship, it is only a minor one. Lisle is more concerned with improving the quality of life and improving the chance for peace by giving volunteers an "... opportunity to explore the moral and ethical dimensions of social interaction and world issues." For this reason potential volunteers should be aware of the philosophical demands placed on all participants.

Lochty Private Railway

Lochty Farm, Near Crail
Fife, Scotland
tel. (0334) 54815

Project Location: Lochty Private Railway, Scotland.
Project Type: Preservation of railway equipment collection, and operating railway.
Project Costs: Membership in Fife Railway Preservation Group.
Project Dates: Generally weekends, but an occasional midweek work force. Information will be supplied upon request.
How To Apply: Send to Fife Railway Preservation Group, 23 Millfield, Cupar, Fife KY15 5UT, Scotland, for more information and application forms.
Work Done by Volunteers: General maintenance of railway during "closed" season, and operating the trains during operating season.
Special Skills or Requirements: A generally keen interest in railways and any skills for any department are welcome.

Los Ninos

1330 Continental St.
San Ysidro CA 92073
tel. (619) 661-6912

Project Locations: Tijuana and Mexicali, Mexico.
Project Types: Los Ninos is an educational program that involves teaching in a summer school and receiving lectures and workshops about the reality of Mexico.
Project Costs: $660 per summer, which includes housing, food, and use of Los Ninos vehicles.
Project Dates: Early July to mid-August.
How To Apply: Contact the above address for application. The deadline each year is late April.
Work Done by Volunteers: Teaching in a summer school and sharing responsibilities while living in a community setting.
Special Skills or Requirements: Participants should have cultural sensitivity, ability to communicate in Spanish, ability to work in a team as well as independently, and be in good health.
Commentary: Los Ninos was formed in 1974, and offers short-term volunteer development training through the Cross-Cultural Interaction program.
Sample Projects: The Tijuana program lasts six weeks, from early July to mid-August, and the Mexicali programs are one week long. There are also occasional construction projects where groups who wish to come for one or two weeks raise funds ($2,000 to $5,000) to cover construction costs, and then help with the construction during their stay in Tijuana.

Macon Program for Progress, Inc.

38½ E. Main St.
PO Box 700
Franklin NC 28734
tel. (704) 524-4471

Project Location: Franklin, North Carolina, which is in the mountains of western North Carolina and surrounded by the Great Smoky Mountains National Park.

Project Type: MPP is a local social service organization.

Project Costs: Volunteers are responsible for all expenses.

Project Dates: Anytime of the year, but summer is the busiest time for the agency.

How To Apply: Send to Teresa Mallonee, Volunteer Coordinator, at the above address, for information and application form.

Work Done by Volunteers: Wide variety of activities, from summer daycare for children, to adult daycare, to building homes for the needy.

Special Skills or Requirements: A desire to work.

Commentary: Volunteers get an opportunity to do needed work, and they also have one of the most scenic vacation spots in the U.S. to spend their free time.

Mellemfolkeligt Samvirke (MS)

Borgergade 10–141300
Copenhagen K., Denmark
tel. 01 32 62 44

Project Locations: Denmark, the Faroe Islands, and Greenland.
Project Type: Workcamps.
Project Costs: 600 Danish kroner.
Project Dates: July and August.
How To Apply: Contact the above address for information on U.S. partner organizations to apply through.
Work Done by Volunteers: Manual labor and social work.
Special Skills or Requirements: No special skills required, but volunteers must be able and willing to work in a multicultural setting.
Commentary: Minimum age for volunteers is 18. All volunteers receive boarding and lodging, but they are responsible for all transportation costs.
Sample Projects: Camps are organized in cooperation with local municipalities and institutions. Typical projects consist of construction of playgrounds, building community centers, restoration of local sites, and nature conservation.

Mencap Holiday Services

119 Drake St.
Rochdale OL16 1PZ, England
tel. 0706-54111

Project Locations: Holidays are in borrowed premises at many sites throughout England.

Project Types: Programs for mentally handicapped people of all ages who live at home or in hospital settings.

Project Costs: Volunteers are reimbursed up to 15 pounds for travel, and room and board is provided.

Project Dates: During summer months for two weeks.

How To Apply: Write to Mencap Holiday Services at the above address for details and application form.

Work Done by Volunteers: Volunteers are responsible for all the personal care needs of the handicapped vacationers. This ranges from washing, dressing, or changing diapers to helping them enjoy their vacation setting. The work is long and hard. The days are often as long as 14 hours, and on a 2-week holiday volunteers can expect to have only a half-day plus late evenings off.

Special Skills or Requirements: A strong commitment to helping the handicapped. Special skills such as music and arts & crafts are a plus. Most volunteers are between 18 and 25, but there is no upper age limit. If you are fit, persevering, and have a responsible attitude toward demanding work you are welcome.

Commentary: While volunteers don't have much time off to tour the countryside, they do have an opportunity to make many friends while doing valuable work. This can be a true change of pace, and the vacation can come afterward.

The Mendenhall Ministries

PO Box 368
Mendenhall MS 39114
tel. (601) 847-3421

Project Location: Mendenhall, Mississippi, in the delta region of the state.

Project Type: Outreach work in a Christian community organization.

Project Costs: Volunteers are responsible for all travel costs and some of room and board.

Project Dates: Anytime during the year as needed by TMM.

How To Apply: Write to Volunteer Coordinator, The Mendenhall Ministries, at the above address, for more information and application form.

Work Done by Volunteers: At present, short- term and summer volunteers do the following: bible training, farm work, legal internships, office work, recreation, research, photography, and tutoring.

Special Skills or Requirements: TMM is a nondenominational, community-based organization, but it has strong connections to a local fundamentalist church, and expects all volunteers to join in group activities, which are based on a strong Christian faith.

Commentary: TMM is a cross-cultural organization with strong ties to the local black community as well as to the Christian community, and volunteers should be willing to participate willingly in both.

Mennonite Central Committee—Canada

134 Plaza Dr.
Winnipeg, Man. R3T 5K9, Canada
tel. (204) 261-6381

Project Locations: Throughout Canada.
Project Types: Mostly social service assignments, which may include childcare, community services, handicapped services, justice advocacy, offender ministries, or youth work.
Project Costs: Volunteers receive food, housing, and $50 monthly allowance. They are responsible for all transportation costs, although limited transportation allowances are given for certain isolated sites.
Project Dates: Summer assignments run from the beginning of May until the end of August, with projects lasting from two to four months.
How To Apply: Send to Mennonite Central Committee—Canada, Summer Service, at the above address, for more information and personal information form.
Work Done by Volunteers: Promoting gardening, day-camp counseling, assisting in a global gift shop, coordinating playground activities, assisting in providing computer services, working with youth in a group home, assisting people with handicaps, and managing a housing complex for low-income families are all activities done by volunteers.
Special Skills or Requirements: Most assignments require at least completion of high school. "A flexible, learning, caring and adventuresome spirit is a definite asset." Active membership in a Christian church is also required, although it doesn't have to be Mennonite.
Commentary: The Mennonite Church began as a radical, Protestant movement in Europe in the sixteenth century. Mennonites believe that faith lives through caring for, sharing with, and serving those suffering from hardship, disadvantage, or oppression. This includes strong commitment to actively seeking justice and making peace. Volunteers, although not required to belong to a Mennonite church, are

expected to commit themselves to these perspectives.

Sample Projects: The Native Gardening Project promotes gardening and fosters relationships in native communities that have invited the MCC's participation. Locations for the project may include remote locations of the Yukon, Northwest Territories, British Columbia, Alberta, Saskatchewan, Manitoba, and Ontario. It gives volunteers an opportunity to do more than just talk about peace, and participants can join Native Canadians in rediscovering what it means to make peace with the earth. Participants are given the opportunity of seeing their own culture through the eyes of others. The attitudes, perceptions, and lives of those who volunteer in a native community may change as a result of the experience.

Midwest Medical Mission, Inc.

c/o Dr. Michael Rench
5757 Monclova Rd.
Maumee OH 43537
tel. (419) 389-1239

Project Location: Dominican Republic.

Project Type: Medical care.

Project Costs: Approximately $1,000 for physicians, and somewhat less for nonphysician medical personnel.

Project Dates: Teams go to the Dominican Republic at various times during the year for a three- or four- week period.

How To Apply: Send to Midwest Medical Mission, Inc., at the above address, for current information and application.

Work Done by Volunteers: Teams of medical personnel work in the Dominican Republic, which is one of the poorest nations in this hemisphere.

Special Skills or Requirements: Most volunteers are licensed doctors, nurses, or technicians, but there are a limited number of positions for people who are willing to work as "gophers" to help the medical team work more smoothly during their short, but extremely busy, stay.

Commentary: Medical help is always needed in Third World countries, and this is one program that uses non- medical volunteers.

Robert Schilling: Participant Extraordinaire

Call Robert Schilling's house and be prepared to leave a message. Don't take it personally if it takes him a year or so to respond. Consider his 1990 schedule: January in Sao Paulo; March in Buenos Aires; May in Hong Kong; June in Malawi; July in Brazil; August in Bolivia; October in Madagascar.

Schilling is not an airline pilot nor an international spy. He's not a bird or a plane. He's a super-participant.

As a veteran of 13 University Research Expeditions Program (UREP) projects, Robert Schilling is one of the program's most intrepid and tireless participants. A retired assistant school superintendent from southern California, Schilling says he has traveled all his life and wanted to avoid the "tunnel vision" he sees many retired educators develop. "I want to contribute to mankind, to do more than play golf or talk about my grandchildren," he said.

Schilling's first UREP expedition was a study of viszcacha (a rabbit-size cousin of the chinchilla) in La Pampa, Argentina. A nasty spider bite landed Schilling in a hospital early in the expedition, but did not dampen his enthusiasm. "Even the 'bad' experiences are valuable," he says. "I made several friends while recovering and still managed to learn more than I ever dreamed about the viszcacha."

Schilling's fluent Spanish has placed Latin America countries among his favorite destinations. He returns to some research sites year after year to renew close friendships made with local researchers and residents.

"The most important elements for an expedition are good

UREP participants take a break on an archaeology expedition in Sardinia, Italy. (Photo courtesy of UREP)

leadership and the chemistry of the group. The chemistry is impossible to predict, but UREP project leaders are exceptional."

Schilling's recent expedition adventures have included UREP projects investigating agricultural methods in Malawi, child nutrition in northeastern Brazil, and festive costumes in the Bolivian Andes.

In early 1990, he had already booked an expedition for January 1991.

Leave a message at the tone and he'll get back to you in a year or so.

This article was originally published in UREP Fieldnotes.

Mingan Island Cetacean Study, Inc.

285 Green
St. Lambert, QC J4P 1T3, Canada
tel. (514) 465-9176

Project Locations: Mingan Island, in the Gulf of St. Lawrence, and Loreto, Baja California.

Project Type: Marine mammal research with emphasis on rorquals.

Project Costs: Volunteers are responsible for transportation to the project, and approximately $115 per day at project to cover research and living costs.

Project Dates: Various times during the year. Generally between June and October at Mingan Island, and around March in Baja California.

How To Apply: Write or call the above-listed office.

Work Done by Volunteers: Assisting scientists in research as required.

Special Skills or Requirements: Some experience handling or working on boats. A degree in biology is required for full assistants.

Commentary: MICS is best known as the first organization in the world to carry out long-term studies on the blue whale.

Sample Projects: Photo-identification of blue, fin, humpback, and minke whales to help determine the distribution, migration patterns, population estimates, behavioral attributes, and genetic makeup of the various populations.

Missouri Department of Natural Resources

Division of Parks, Recreation, and Historic Preservation
PO Box 176
Jefferson City MO 65102
tel. (314) 751-2479 or (800) 334-6946

Project Location: Statewide in Missouri state parks and state historic sites.

Project Types: Campground host, interpreter, park aide, and trail work.

Project Costs: Volunteers are responsible for all travel and living expenses, although they may stay in park- owned housing, or camp at no cost if facilities are available.

Project Dates: Mid-May to mid-September for hosts and interpreters. Park aide and trail work positions may be year-round.

How To Apply: Contact Volunteer Program Coordinator at the phone and address given above.

Work Done by Volunteers: The above-mentioned jobs are done by volunteers, who are expected to perform at the same standards as paid employees. Volunteers are scheduled according to volunteer availability and park needs.

Special Skills or Requirements: Physical ability to perform assigned tasks. Campground hosts serve a minimum of four weeks.

Mobility International U.S.A.

PO Box 3551
Eugene OR 97403
tel. (503) 343-1284 (voice and TDD)

Project Locations: MIUSA sponsors workcamps in Oregon, helps place people with disabilities in workcamps in the U.S. and abroad.

Project Types: Normal workcamp experiences, plus social service organizations. International educational exchange programs with the intention of increasing international understanding of the disabled are also part of MIUSA's program.

Project Costs: Vary according to the program.

Project Dates: Workcamp dates vary, but most are for two to four weeks.

How To Apply: Send a stamped, self-addressed envelope to Mobility International U.S.A. at the above address for information on workcamps and other programs.

Work Done by Volunteers: Exchange programs usually include a community service component. Service projects have involved making trails in national forests, a city park in Costa Rica, a retreat center accessible to wheelchair users and visually impaired people, and volunteering in agencies and organizations offering services to people with disabilities.

Special Skills or Requirements: MIUSA prefers people, able-bodied or disabled, with an interest and/or expertise in independent living for people with disabilities. Specific requirements vary with project.

Commentary: Mobility International was founded in London in 1973 to integrate persons with disabilities into international educational and travel programs. Today it has offices in more than 25 countries; MIUSA's U.S. headquarters became active in 1981. MIUSA also publishes several books, including a recently updated version of *A World of Options: A Guide to International Educational Exchange, Community Service and Travel for Persons With Disabilities.* They also offer the *Manual for Integrating People With Disabilities into International Educational Exchange Programs.* Also available are the videos "Looking Back, Looking Forward," and "Mi Casa Es Su Casa," which document the experiences of former MIUSA volunteers.

Mount Shasta Trail

Mount Shasta Ranger District
Mount Shasta CA 96967

Project Location: Mount Shasta, which is in northern California near the Oregon boarder.
Project Type: Trail building.
Project Costs: Volunteers will be responsible for transportation to project and may be responsible for room and board.
Project Dates: To be set.
How To Apply: Write to the above address for more information.
Work Done by Volunteers: All aspects of building trails, most of which will be 6,000–8,000 feet long.
Special Skills or Requirements: Interest in the outdoors and physical stamina.
Commentary: This is a new project that is expected to last between 5 and 10 years. It offers an opportunity to get in on the beginning of a new trail-building project similar to the Colorado and Lake Tahoe Rim Trails.

Mount Vernon Ladies' Association

Archaeology Department
Mount Vernon VA 22121
tel. (703) 780-2000, ext. 326

Project Location: Mount Vernon, Virginia.
Project Types: Archaeological excavation and artifact processing.
Project Costs: Participants must pay all transportation, room, and board.
How To Apply: Contact Dennis Pogue, chief archaeologist, at the above address.
Work Done by Volunteers: Excavation and recording in the field; and artifact washing, labeling, and cataloging in the lab.
Special Skills or Requirements: A willingness to work hard and a time commitment of one day or more.
Commentary: There is a possibility of some volunteer opportunities arising after the summer excavation season.

National Association of Volunteer Bureaux

St. Peter's College
College Rd.
Saltley, Birmingham B8 3TE, England
tel. 021-327-0265

Project Locations: Across the U.K.
Project Types: All types of volunteer work.
Project Costs: Volunteers generally provide for travel, room, and board.
Project Dates: Throughout the year.
How To Apply: Volunteers must apply through a local volunteer agency, but the National Association can put potential volunteers in touch with agencies anywhere in the U.K.
Work Done by Volunteers: A wide variety of work is available.
Special Skills or Requirements: Varies by volunteer opportunity, but generally none.
Commentary: The National Association is an organization of more than 350 local volunteer agencies in the United Kingdom that can provide information for potential volunteers who have little knowledge of the volunteer opportunities that are available around the U.K.

They're Blazing Paths for Others

by Lucinda Dillon

In her hometown of Portsmouth, England, 23-year-old Amanda Bullion can't ride the city bus, she can't watch a movie in a theater, and she can't roll her wheelchair into many public buildings.

Kingstone Kelly Zimba, whose legs were amputated below the knee joints after a train accident 15 years ago, prefers to attach prostheses to his legs. People in his hometown of

Kingstone Kelly Zimba of Zambia (left) and John Baxter of Australia clear vegetation from a trail at Broken Bowl Picnic Area near Fall Creek Reservoir in Oregon. (Photo courtesy of Andy Nelson)

Lusaka, Zambia stare mercilessly when he uses his wheelchair.

Bullion and Zimba both want to advance opportunities for people in their countries who have disabilities. They were a part of a 31-person international delegation that visited Eugene, Oregon in 1989 as part of a leadership exchange program sponsored by Mobility International U.S.A.

They worked at the Broken Bowl Picnic Area in the Willamette National Forest, 35 miles southeast of Eugene. There they widened paths, restructured picnic areas, and otherwise made campsites more accessible to people with disabilities.

"I came here to see how far Eugene has come and how these other people are getting things across in their countries," said Bullion, who was born with cerebral palsy, "I've got to go back and tell other disabled people."

The delegates, most of whom are disabled, learned about themselves and each other during the four-day community project in the forest, and they shared experiences and suggestions.

Zimba camped outdoors for the first time—one of several new experiences he had in Eugene.

"When I came to Eugene, I couldn't believe my eyes—I can get on the bus here and get around anywhere," said Zimba, who is deputy chief executive of administration for the Zambian Council for the Handicapped.

While Zimba and Bullion clipped, raked, and pruned back the growth along paved trails to allow passage of standard 32-inch wheelchairs, other delegates worked to elevate ground-level barbecue pits to a height more accessible to people using wheelchairs.

Efforts to make the campsites "barrier free" were long overdue, said Chuck Frayer, accessibility/engineering specialist for the U.S. Forest Service, who visited the site.

"Until recently, the Forest Service really hasn't done much marketing of services for the disabled," he said. "We're learning that what we thought was accessible really wasn't accessible."

So the partnership with Mobility International U.S.A.

(MIUSA), which has completed several similar projects within the forest, is a valuable one, he said.

MIUSA is the Eugene-based, U.S. branch of Mobility International, a 23-nation organization. The group promotes international understanding and provides opportunities for people with disabilities to exchange information that will improve their lives, said its director, Susan Sygall.

The exchanges generate a "powerful connection" among disabled people who have similar challenges, goals, and experiences, she said.

"There's a real sense of solidarity," Sygall said. "They were all here with a mission—to improve services in their country."

Workshops highlighted topics including leadership skills, discrimination, and sexuality.

"Every disabled person, no matter what country they're from, has experienced some form of discrimination," Sygall said.

One woman in the group once was turned away from a resort because of her disability. Another was denied an airline reservation. Eleven people in the group use wheelchairs.

Bullion resents that she can't go to the theater and must wait for her favorite movies to come out on videotape. "We're a fire hazard," she says.

Similarly, Ryan Tu, 25, believes business owners in Taipei, Taiwan, have passed him up for jobs because he walks with a limp.

"Sometimes you don't even get to talk to the boss because when you come in, the staff sees how you walk and thinks you can't do the job," said Tu, whose leg is affected by nerve damage that he suffered during a knee operation.

As a volunteer for the National Society of Rehabilitation for the Republic of China, Tu hopes to support laws ensuring employment equality for people with disabilities. "People think it's cruel to make the disabled do some kind of job, but it's even crueler not to let them," he said.

This article first appeared in The Register-Guard *of Eugene, Oregon on July 12, 1989.*

National Audubon Society

950 Third Ave.
New York NY 10022
tel. (212) 832-3200

The national office of the Audubon Society does not place volunteers, but regional offices and local clubs often have programs where volunteers are used. Volunteers work on projects such as habitat restoration and trail building, or as guides and visitor center workers. You can obtain information from the regional offices listed below about activities being conducted by local clubs.

Mid-Atlantic Region
1104 Fernwood Ave., Suite 300
Camp Hill PA 17011
tel. (717) 763-4985

Northeast Region
1789 Western Ave.
Albany NY 12203
tel. (518) 869-9731

Southeast Region
928 N. Monroe St.
Tallahassee FL 32303
tel. (904) 222-2473

Great Lakes Region
7 N. Meridian St., #400
Indianapolis IN 46204
tel. (317) 631-2676

West Central Region
200 Southwind Pl., #205
Manhattan KS 66502
tel. (913) 537-4385

Southwest Region
2525 Wallingwood, #1505
Austin TX 78746
tel. (512) 327-1943

Rocky Mountain Region
4150 Darley, Suite 5
Boulder CO 80303
tel. (303) 499-0219

Western Region
2631 12th Ct., SW, #A
Olympia WA 98502
tel. (206) 786-8020

Alaska and Hawaii
308 G St., Suite 217
Anchorage AK 99501
tel. (907) 276-7034

National Park Service
Interior Bldg.
PO Box 37127
Washington DC 20013-7127
tel. (202) 343-6843

Some regions of the National Park Service have individual
entries, but you can also contact any of the regional offices
listed below for a list of volunteer openings.

Mid-Atlantic Region
143 S. Third St.
Philadelphia PA 19106
tel. (215) 597-7013

North Atlantic Region
15 State St.
Boston MA 02109
tel. (617) 223-3769

Southeast Region
75 Spring St., SW
Atlanta GA 30303
tel. (404) 221-5185

Midwest Region
1709 Jackson St.
Omaha NE 68102
tel. (402) 221-3431

Southwest Region
Old Santa Fe Trail
PO Box 728
Santa Fe NM 87501
tel. (505) 988-6388

Rocky Mountain Region
PO Box 25287
Denver CO 80225
tel. (303) 236-8700

Western Region
450 Golden Gate Ave.
PO Box 36063
San Francisco CA 94102
tel. (415) 556-4196

Pacific Northwest Region
1920 Westin Bldg.
2001 Sixth Ave.
Seattle WA 98121
tel. (206) 442-5565

National Capital
1100 Ohio Dr., SW
Washington DC 20242
tel. (202) 426-6612

Alaska
2525 Gambell St., Room 107
Anchorage AK 99503
tel. (907) 261-2690

National Park Service—Mid-Atlantic Region

143 S. Third St.
Philadelphia PA 19106
tel. (215) 597-5374

Project Locations: Pennsylvania, Virginia, West Virginia, Delaware, and Maryland.

Project Types: Visitors' services, campground host, administrative support, and research in history, archaeology, and natural sciences.

Project Costs: NPS pays for some out-of- pocket expenses for volunteers, but volunteers are responsible for most housing and transportation costs.

Project Dates: Year-round.

How To Apply: Send to the above address for a "Prospective Volunteer Application" and a list of parks under the mid-Atlantic region.

Work Done by Volunteers: Providing visitors with information on what to see and do during their visits, assisting park staff in continuing research, participating in wildlife surveys, and doing regular maintenance work.

Special Skills or Requirements: Special skills and interests are helpful, but parks are willing to help train volunteers for specific needs.

Commentary: More than 116,600 volunteer hours were donated by over 3,000 volunteers in the mid-Atlantic region in 1987. That is equivalent to over 60 full-time employees for one year.

National Park Service—
Rocky Mountain Region

12795 W. Alameda Pkwy., Box 25287
Denver CO 80225-0287
tel. 969-2630

Project Locations: National parks and monuments in Colorado, Montana, North Dakota, South Dakota, Utah, and Wyoming.

Project Types: Campground hosts, visitor center information desks, plant and animal surveys, living history demonstrations, and artifact preservations.

Project Costs: Volunteers are responsible for transportation, food, and housing, although with some positions housing is furnished.

Project Dates: Generally May to September, with most projects lasting between 4 and 12 weeks.

How To Apply: Write or call Douglas Caldwell, Volunteer Coordinator, at the above address.

Work Done by Volunteers: Office work, campground maintenance, trail maintenance, museum work, and staffing information desks.

Special Skills or Requirements: Varies by park needs. Generally volunteers should have experience or interest in camping, hiking, backcountry skills, public speaking, history, geology, or archaeology.

Commentary: Some openings require specialized skills such as photography, computer programming, spelunking, or experience in any of these interest areas.

Sample Projects: Monitoring threatened plant and animal species, providing general information to park visitors, geyser gazing, cave research, and recording research information on computers.

The Nature Conservancy

1815 N. Lynn St.
Arlington VA 22209
tel. (703) 841-5300

Although The Nature Conservancy asks that you not contact its national headquarters about volunteer opportunities, the state chapters listed below often need volunteers who help with habitat restoration and docent work at various preserves, and you are welcome to apply to the states of your choice.

Alaska Field Office
300 W. Fifth Ave., Suite 550
Anchorage AK 99501
tel. (907) 276-3133

Arizona Field Office
300 E. University Blvd., Suite 230
Tucson AZ 85705
tel. (602) 622-3861

Arkansas Field Office
300 Spring Bldg., Suite 717
Little Rock AR 72201
tel. (501) 372-2750

California Field Office
785 Market St.
San Francisco CA 94103
tel. (415) 777-0487

Colorado Field Office
1244 Pine St.
Boulder CO 80302
tel. (303) 444-2950

Connecticut Chapter
55 High St.
Middletown CT 06457
tel. (203) 344-0716

Florida Field Office
1353 Palmetto Ave.
Winter Park FL 32789
tel. (407) 628-5887

Georgia Field Office
4725 Peachtree Corners Circle, Suite 395
Norcross GA 30092
tel. (404) 263-9225

Hawaii Field Office
1116 Smith St., Suite 201
Honolulu HI 96817
tel. (808) 537-4508

Idaho Field Office
PO Box 64
Sun Valley ID 83353
tel. (208) 726-3007

Illinois Field Office
79 West Monroe St., Suite 708
Chicago IL 60603
tel. (312) 346-8166

Indiana Field Office
4200 N. Michigan Rd.
Indianapolis IN 46208
tel. (317) 923-7547

Iowa Field Office
431 E. Locust, Suite 200
Des Moines IA 50309
tel. (515) 244-5044

Kentucky Chapter
324 West Main St.
Frankfort KY 40601
tel. (502) 875-3529

Louisiana Field Office
PO Box 4125
Baton Rouge LA 70821
tel. (504) 338-1040

Maine Chapter
122 Main St.
Topsham ME 04086
tel. (207) 729-5181

Maryland/Delaware Field Office
Chevy Chase Metro Bldg.
2 Wisconsin Circle, Suite 410
Chevy Chase MD 20815
tel. (301) 656-8673

Massachusetts Field Office
294 Washington St., Room 740
Boston MA 02108
tel. (617) 423-2545

Michigan Field Office
2840 East Grand River, Suite 5
East Lansing MI 48823
tel. (517) 332-1741

Minnesota/Great Plains Field Office
1313 Fifth St., SE
Minneapolis MN 55414
tel. (612) 379-2134

Missouri Field Office
2800 S. Brentwood Blvd.
St. Louis MO 63144
tel. (314) 968-1105

Montana/Wyoming Field Office
Last Chance Gulch and Sixth
PO Box 258
Helena MT 59624
tel. (406) 443-0303

Nebraska Field Office
LeDioyt Landmark
1001 Farnam-on-the-Mall
Omaha NE 68102
tel. (402) 342-0282

New Hampshire Field Office
5 South State St., Suite 1A
Concord NH 03301
tel. (603) 224-5853

New Jersey Field Office
17 Fairmont Road
PO Box 181
Pottersville NJ 07979-0181
tel. (201) 439-3007

New Mexico Field Office
107 Cienega St.
Santa Fe NM 87501
tel. (505) 988-3867

New York Field Office
1736 Western Ave.
Albany NY 12203
tel. (518) 869-6959

North Carolina Field Office
Carr Mill, Suite 223
Carrboro NC 27510
tel. (919) 967-7007

Ohio Field Office
1504 W. First Ave.
Columbus OH 43212
tel. (614) 486-6789

Oklahoma Field Office
320 S. Boston, Suite 846
Tulsa OK 74103
tel. (918) 585-1117

Oregon Field Office
1205 NW 25th Ave.
Portland OR 97210
tel. (503) 228-9561

Pennsylvania Field Office
1218 Chestnut St., Suite 807
Philadelphia PA 19107
tel. (215) 925-1065

Rhode Island Field Office
294 Washington St., Room 740
Boston MA 02108
tel. (617) 423-2545

South Carolina Field Office
PO Box 5475
Columbia SC 29250
tel. (803) 254-9049

Tennessee Field Office
PO Box 3017
Nashville TN 37219
tel. (615) 242-1787

Texas Field Office
PO Box 1440
San Antonio TX 78295-1440
tel. (512) 224-8774

Utah/Great Basin Field Office
PO Box 11486, Pioneer Station
Salt lake City UT 84102
tel. (801) 531-0999

Vermont Field Office
138 Main St.
Montpelier VT 05602
tel. (802) 229-4425

Virginia Field Office
1110 Rose Hill Dr., Suite 200
Charlottesville VA 22901
tel. (804) 295-6106

Washington Field Office
1601 Second Ave., Suite 910
Seattle WA 98101
tel. (206) 728-9696

West Virginia Field Office
922 Quarrier St., Suite 414
Charleston WV 25301
tel. (304) 345-4350

Wisconsin Field Office
1045 E. Dayton St., Room 209
Madison WI 53703
tel. (608) 251-8140

Nevada Division of State Parks

201 S. Fall St., Room 119
Carson City NV 89710
tel. (702) 885-4384

Project Locations: Throughout Nevada.

Project Types: Trail workers, campground hosts, interpretive assistants, and other common park positions.

Project Costs: Volunteers responsible for all transportation and living costs.

Project Dates: Year-round for varying lengths of stay.

How To Apply: Send for the *Volunteer in Park* bulletin at the above address for information on what positions are available and application form.

Work Done by Volunteers: All types of work are done by volunteers, from hosting campgrounds, to surveying archaeological digs, to patrolling the backcountry.

Special Skills or Requirements: Some positions require special skills, and these are specified in the bulletin.

Commentary: As with most state park systems, Nevada depends a lot on volunteers to keep its system going.

New York–New Jersey Trail Conference

232 Madison Ave., #908
New York NY 10016
tel. (212) 685-9699

Project Location: Northern New Jersey, from the Delaware Water Gap to the Catskills, and Taconics in southern New York.

Project Types: Trail building, repair, and management.

Project Costs: Volunteers are responsible for all food and transportation costs.

Project Dates: Projects run year-round, usually for one day, but sometimes for the weekend.

How To Apply: Contact Trail Conference at the above address.

Work Done by Volunteers: Clipping and clearing trails, painting blazes, cleaning water bars and bridges, draining ditches, and rehabilitating trails.

Special Skills or Requirements: Should be reasonably fit, and a knowledge of trail tools would be helpful.

Sample Projects: Constructing 58-foot bridge over a stream and an elevated boardwalk over a fragile area, draining ditches, and clearing trails.

Nicaragua Solidarity Network

339 Lafayette St.
New York NY 10012
tel. (212) 674-9499

Project Locations: The five boroughs of New York City.
Project Types: Activist activities.
Project Costs: Participants are responsible for travel, room, and board expenses.
Project Dates: Year-round.
How To Apply: Send resume and cover letter to the above address.
Work Done by Volunteers: Media networking, outreach, street theater, fund-raising, and producing a monthly newsletter.
Special Skills or Requirements: Volunteers should be familiar with Central American issues, and interested in the progressive solidarity movement.

Northern Ohio Archaeological Field School

Cuyahoga Community College
11000 Pleasant Valley Rd.
Parma OH 44130
tel. (216) 987-5492

Project Location: Cuyahoga Valley, Ohio.
Project Type: Archaeological excavation.
Project Costs: From $25 to $60 per week, plus room and board.
Project Dates: From late June to early August for two to six weeks.
How To Apply: Send to the above address for application form.
Work Done by Volunteers: Archaeological excavation and class training.
Special Skills or Requirements: None, but an interest in archaeology.
Commentary: This field school excavates both prehistoric Native American and historic nineteenth-century archaeological sites.
Sample Projects: One recent project of the field school has been to conduct research on the life in the 1870s, in the Irishtown Bend section of Cleveland.

North York Moors Historical Railway Trust

The Station
Pickering, North Yorkshire YO18 7AJ, England
tel. 0751-72508

Project Location: Along an 18-mile railway.

Project Types: All aspects of railway maintenance and operations.

Project Costs: Volunteers are provided sleeping accommodations in coaches. Food and travel costs are the responsibility of volunteers.

Project Dates: The railway prefers to have volunteers between late March and September.

How To Apply: Write to General Manager at the above address.

Work Done by Volunteers: Painting, drainage, lineside clearance, landscaping, and minor building repair are all examples of volunteer work.

Special Skills or Requirements: All volunteers should be physically fit. Anyone with technical and/or railway experience may be given opportunities for skilled jobs.

Commentary: Visiting groups may undertake special projects by arrangement. In 1986 and 1987 a group of volunteers from the British Trust for Conservation completed fencing, drainage, and bridge painting projects.

Bangladesh Experience

by Ken Gaebler

Recently, the country of Bangladesh found itself in the grip of flooding that put three-quarters of the country under water. By most official estimates this was one of the worst natural disasters of this century.

For many of us, this front-page news was dismissed as a minor issue, to be glanced at en route to the comics or sports sections. For me the articles were read cringingly and painfully. Hoping for the best, each day brought the worst: "home washed away . . . spreading of water-borne disease . . . isolation from adequate medical treatment . . . inadequate food supply."

Nearly a year before I had left the States for Bangladesh to participate in the 1987 winter workcamps there. I am miles away from Bangladesh, but it is still with me. Hardly a day goes by when I do not reflect back on my memories of the camps. The experience was profound and enlightening, the lessons learned infinitely more valuable than any formal education that I have undergone.

Can you imagine what the second poorest country in the world is like? Could you survive on the Bangladesh average annual per capita income of less than $140? Would you tolerate illiteracy, homelessness, lack of basic sanitation and hygiene, nonexistent medical facilities, and inadequate educational facilities? How would you function under an unstable, despotic government that encourages a political and economic substructure where indeed the rich get richer and the poor get poorer? Remember again the floods—would you survive the seasonal natural disasters that plague Bangladesh?

Raped for centuries by oppressive imperialists, Bangladesh only received its independence in 1971. My friend Amdahd tearfully explained to me that this was a war of genocide in which atrocious murders were committed by what is now Pakistan. His whole family was murdered. This story was repeated to me numerous times by others I met. Is it any wonder that there is now a dearth of new leadership?

Meet Hafiz. His crops destroyed by floods last year, Hafiz was forced to sell his small parcel of land to feed his family. Pursuing that omnipresent dream of emigration, Hafiz gave his life savings to a questionable businessman who promised a visa to Saudi Arabia for Hafiz and his family. Neither the businessman nor the visas were ever seen again. To feed his family, Hafiz left his family. He now works as a cook, a hundred miles away from what once was his home, earning a mere pittance, most of which he sends to his now homeless family.

Many of the Bangladeshi SCI volunteers we worked with were college students. While we were in Bangladesh, nationwide strikes were declared as a protest against President Ershad's government. The country stopped functioning and we were required to stay inside all day. Often, the camps were delayed or canceled. This gave us the opportunity to talk about issues. We learned that this political chaos had been commonplace for many years. In fact, the college students we worked with were often seven years into their four-year degrees. For the past three years, the government had shut down all colleges because the colleges bred a strong voice of political protest against the incumbent Ershad. Again while we were there, the universities were shut down.

The magnitude of the social, economic, meteorological, and political injustices faced by Bangladesh is mind-boggling, to say the least.

Yet the Bangladeshi people bear their misfortunes with dignity. I can't remember ever seeing so many happy faces before. Everyone we worked with was friendly and outgoing. We especially enjoyed nightly sing-a-long sessions. We realized that although Bangladesh is a poor country, its culture is rich.

By bringing people together to share such simple things as singing a song or playing a game of badminton, the SCI workcamps demonstrated that people are people, and they are all the same when you cut through racial and geographical barriers. There was a strong feeling of international solidarity in the camps. We questioned the value of this solidarity, this sense of a global community helping each other, and decided that in the end if enough people felt the same way things would change for the better.

I left Bangladesh confused. I had expected to find answers to some questions. How is it that we allow the inequalities between First and Third World countries to exist? What are the causes? What is the best way to solve the problems and remove the injustices? Why is it that it takes the worst natural disaster of the century to bring a Bangladesh to the front page? Shouldn't the unjust structures that currently exist in our society be first and foremost on all of our minds—on the front pages every day until the problems are solved?

Throughout the camps, the questions persisted. While digging the fish ponds, planting the gardens, building the community toilet facilities, assisting with the cataract operations, and visiting other organizations' projects, I continued to wrestle with these issues, bouncing each new thought off my fellow workcampers.

In the end the answers didn't come. What came was a raising of my consciousness—a spark of desire to do what I saw many others doing. After seeing so many people working to help others I saw for myself that I could contribute. To go to Bangladesh I had taken a leave of absence from an upwardly mobile job where I took things for granted. It took a trip to Bangladesh with SCI as a catalyst to make me realize exactly what I took for granted, and you can bet that it won't happen again. For this, I am indebted to SCI. My biggest hope is that others will follow in my footsteps and seek this same awakening.

This article was published by Service Civil International/U.S.A. in their fall 1988 newsletter Workcamp News.

Only one or two experienced volunteers who are familiar with SCI and who will work with the organization upon their return are sent to Asian countries each year.

Nothelfergemeinschaft der Freunde e.v.

Auf der Kornerwiese 5
6000 Frankfurt/Main, 1 Germany

Project Locations: Throughout Germany and Europe.
Project Type: Workcamps.
Project Costs: Approximately $25 registration fee, plus transportation costs.
Project Dates: Spring and summer for U.S. volunteers.
How To Apply: Write to Paul Krahe at the above address for more information and application form. Application deadline is April 30.
Work Done by Volunteers: Volunteers spend three to four weeks working in regions hit by catastrophe or economic depression. They may help with construction of public buildings or help counsel people affected by some disaster.
Special Skills or Requirements: None, but an interest in people and international exchange.
Commentary: Workcamp volunteers are supervised by group leaders who are former workcamp volunteers, and who have attended workcamp leader seminars.

Oceanic Society Expeditions

Fort Mason Center, Suite E-240
San Francisco CA 94123
tel. (415) 441-1106 or (800) 326-7491

Project Locations: Current projects are under way in the Bahamas and southeast Alaska, with a new project being considered in the Peruvian Amazon.

Project Types: Research in the social/family structure and behavior of free-ranging dolphins. Also photo-identification of humpback whales.

Project Costs: Costs vary from $1,150 for Project Dolphin, in the Bahamas, to $2,490 for the Southeast Alaska Humpback Whale Expedition.

Project Dates: The Bahamas Dolphin project runs from May through August, with weekly departures. The Southeast Alaska Humpback Whale Expedition is generally held for the first two weeks of August. The new project in the Amazon will generally run the last part of June if it is approved.

How To Apply: Call or write to the above address for application forms.

Work Done by Volunteers: In the Bahamas, volunteers, working under the guidance of field biologists, will snorkel among wild spotted dolphins in the Bahamas Banks. They will photograph and videotape the dolphins to record spot patterns for identification of individual dolphins. This will assist volunteers in recording data about age, sex, and various social behaviors. Volunteers in southeast Alaska will photograph humpback whales from aboard a research vessel, as well as collect phyloplankton and zooplankton samples. Volunteers on the Amazon River project will do much the same things as those in the Bahamas, except they will be investigating the activities of Amazon River dolphins.

Special Skills or Requirements: All expeditions require that volunteers have an adventurous spirit, respect for wildlife, and the ability to follow instructions. Basic snorkeling and swimming skills are required for the projects in the Bahamas and the Amazon.

Commentary: Project Dolphin (Bahamas) is a 20-year research project undertaken by the Oceanic Society to gather multi-generational baseline data on a group of free-ranging spotted dolphins. The Amazon project will be similar to the Bahamas one.

Operation Crossroads Africa, Inc.

150 Fifth Ave.
New York NY 10011
tel. (212) 242-8550

Project Locations: Rural Africa and the Caribbean.

Project Types: Crossroads has four major types of projects: (1) community construction, (2) agricultural/farming, (3) archaeology/anthropology, and (4) medical.

Project Costs: $3,250 for Africa and $2,100 for the Caribbean.

Project Dates: Late June to mid-August. African projects are for seven weeks and Caribbean projects are for six weeks.

How To Apply: Write to Crossroads Africa at the above address for more information and application. Application deadline is February 15 each year, but late applicants are often accepted.

Work Done by Volunteers: In Africa, college students work on specialized projects such as medicine, nursing, community development, archaeology, architectural photography, and agriculture. In the Caribbean, high school students work side-by-side with local counterparts constructing medical clinics, schools, and community centers. They also help establish day camps for children.

Special Skills or Requirements: Must be a college student for service in Africa, and a high school or college student to serve in the Caribbean. Crossroads has an extensive screening process and requires a number of references for all applicants. Cross-roads accepts some older volunteers as project leaders.

Commentary: This program was the model that President John Kennedy used for developing the Peace Corps, and it has maintained its high level of volunteer programs since 1958. It's an expensive program for youth, but many volunteers have local organizations such as churches or service clubs help finance their trip. Crossroads gives assistance to volunteers who want to raise funds.

226

Oregon River Experiences, Inc.

18800 NE Trunk Road
Dundee OR 97115-3358
tel. (503) 538-3358

Project Locations: Various rivers in the Northwest, including the Rogue, Grande Ronde, Owyhee, John Day, and Deschutes in Oregon; the Klamath in California; and the Lower Salmon in Idaho.

Project Types: Educational whitewater river trips, many for senior citizens through the Elderhostel program.

Project Costs: Volunteers must pay their own transportation to and from program site, and provide own sleeping bags, tents, and personal gear.

Project Dates: Week-long Elderhostel programs begin most Sundays from mid-May through September, and other programs of three to five days are scheduled from April through September.

How To Apply: Send a letter and resume, summarizing qualifications, background, and experience, to the above address.

Work Done by Volunteers: Volunteers teach college-level minicourses in subjects directly related to the river and the area surrounding it. Typical subjects include geology, botany, ornithology, river ecology, local history, Indian lore, archaeology, astronomy, etc. Lectures should be supported by appropriate handouts furnished by volunteers for 25 students.

Special Skills or Requirements: Volunteers should have excellent verbal teaching skills and must be able to demonstrate a thorough knowledge of the subject. For Elderhostel programs all resumes and support materials will be reviewed by an academic oversight staff at Western Oregon College. These are wilderness camping programs, so all participants should be in good physical condition.

Commentary: Oregon River Experiences has been conducting educational river trips in the Northwest since 1977. They began doing Elderhostel programs in 1986, and have 17 programs scheduled for 1991.

Railway Preservation Society of Ireland

Castleview Rd.
Whitehead, County Antrim BT38 9NA, Northern Ireland

Project Locations: Whitehead, County Antrim, Northern Ireland, and Mullingar, County Westmgath, Eire.

Project Type: Restoration of locomotives—mostly steam, although there are a few diesel—and carriages for railways throughout Ireland.

Project Costs: Volunteers are responsible for room, board, and transportation.

Project Dates: Any weekend throughout the year.

How To Apply: Send to the above address for information and application.

Work Done by Volunteers: Volunteers are involved in all restoration and upkeep activities on the rolling stock on the railways, including major overhauls on the engines.

Special Skills or Requirements: A willingness to work hard and follow instructions.

Commentary: The society, which was formed in 1964, is actively engaged in restoring locomotives and carriages for use on excursion trains. To date, its collection of restored items is comprised of 9 steam locomotives, 2 diesels, over 30 coaches, and a number of rail cars.

Sample Projects: The Society is currently restoring two locomotives. No. 461 is the last survivor of 54 locomotives of the mogul (2-6-0) wheel arrangement that ran in various parts of Ireland. Most of her life was spent hauling heavy freight trains on the steeply graded Wexford-Dublin Line. No. 27 was the last conventional steam locomotive built for the Irish Railways, and is one of only two locomotives with a 0-6-4T wheel arrangement left in the United Kingdom.

Religious Society of Friends

Friends Weekend Workcamps
1515 Cherry St.
Philadelphia PA 19102
tel. (215) 241-7236

Project Location: Philadelphia.
Project Type: Inner-city workcamp.
Project Costs: $35 for weekend workcamp. Volunteers are responsible for all transportation costs.
Project Dates: Weekend camps run monthly from January through May.
How To Apply: Send to Michael Van Hoy, Friends Workcamps, at the above address for more information and application. Weekend camps are limited to 18 participants, so apply early.
Work Done by Volunteers: Wide variety of activities from preparing meals and taking care of children at a shelter for homeless women and children, to visiting elderly people, to helping people repair their homes.
Special Skills or Requirements: Anyone 15 and older can apply for either camp. The Friends attempt to bring together as many people from different backgrounds, races, countries, and states as possible, so applicants from outside the Philadelphia area are encouraged to apply.
Commentary: The weekend workcamps are an excellent way for volunteers to find out about the workcamp experience without making a commitment to go to a foreign land for a longer stay.

Rempart

1, rue des Guillemites
75004 Paris, France
tel. (1) 42 71 96 55

Project Locations: Throughout France at over 150 sites.
Project Type: Archaeological restoration of historical monuments and sites of France.
Project Costs: Vary by site. Some sites provide room and board, while others don't. Volunteers are responsible for all transportation costs.
Project Dates: Most projects are in July and August. Some sites accept volunteers for as little as a weekend, some allow two-week stays, and others require that volunteers stay for the complete two months.
How To Apply: Write to Marie-Jeanne Dallois à la Delegation nationale de l'Union Rempart at the above address for more information and application. If you don't speak French, have an interpreter handy, for they don't send English translations.
Work Done by Volunteers: Wide variety of archaeological excavation work at each site.
Special Skills or Requirements: Volunteers should have at least the rudiments of French, and be interested in both hard work and the archaeology of France.
Commentary: This is the largest organization in France that coordinates the excavation and restoration of historical monuments.

Renaissance du Chateau

77 Fir Hill Tower, Suite 9B2
Akron OH 44304- 1554
tel. (216) 434-9362

Project Locations: Various locations in France.
Project Type: Preservation of historic sites.
Project Costs: $1,400 to $1,600 for either three or four weeks. This price includes round-trip airfare from New York, and room and board in France.
Project Dates: Generally summer.
How To Apply: Write to the above address for application forms and current catalog.
Work Done by Volunteers: Wide variety of archaeological and restoration work. Much of this work is hard physical labor.
Special Skills or Requirements: No special skills are required, and only minimal French is required. Volunteers should be aware, however, that spoken French is an important aspect of the program.
Commentary: This program is based on the tradition of French *chantiers,* or collective efforts, and all are headed by French directors.

Up from the Ashes

Jim Wright of the U.S. Forest Service is in search of a few good volunteers. He needs people who are willing to get down on their hands and knees to grub around newly planted fir and pine trees and tear out competing vegetation, who are physically able to do the back-breaking work of planting those young trees; and those who can do the less demanding, but just as important, job of placing vexar tubing around the seedlings to keep deer and elk from eating them.

None of these jobs, or any of the others available to volunteers through the U.S. Forest Service's Operation Phoenix, offer anything other than food, shelter, tools, supervision, and the satisfaction of helping a national forest recover from one of the most devastating fire seasons ever experienced in California. Nonetheless, in 1989 over 100 men, women, and children volunteered 68,000 hours through Operation Phoenix, planting 8,000 trees, constructing fish habitats and check dams, and rebuilding trails.

I recently toured areas where Operation Phoenix volunteers work, and I wasn't surprised when USFS employee Larry Wernicke said, "Welcome to one of our 'nuked' zones," as he led me down an incline along Yellow Jacket Ridge in the Klamath National Forest, near California's northern border.

If I didn't already know that the conflagration was started by one of the 2,000 lightning strikes that hit the Klamath National Forest in a 20-minute period late on August 30, 1987, I might have taken him literally.

On slopes where mature forests of pine and fir had stood, there was no undergrowth, and nothing left to grow under.

Volunteers move large boulders into place as a base for a new check dam along a mountain stream in the burned-over Klamath National Forest. (Photo courtesy of Bill McMillon)

There was no luxurious growth along stream banks, for plants that had lived even in the damp environment had been burned to their roots. Just ashes and charred remains of gigantic trees.

Not all of the 400 square miles of forest in the Klamath National Forest touched by the 1987 fires were so devastated, but the USFS have labeled nearly 50,000 acres as "intensely burned."

Forest fires are common in California. Some 100,000 acres, mostly brushland in the southern portion of the state, burn each year, but the dry lightning storms that traveled the length of the state from south to north in 1987 started a siege of fire that burned more than 800,000 acres of forestland before it was quenched by the winter rains that began to fall in November.

And 250,000 of those acres were in one national forest, the Klamath.

After the strikes on August 30, the Klamath fires spread slowly but unchecked over the mountain ridges and down the canyons. Few fire fighters were available when the first flames soared above the treetops because all available personnel had already been sent south to fight fires in the Stanislaus and Mendocino National Forests.

This gave between 150 and 200 small fires ignited by the

An Operation Phoenix volunteer drives willow stakes into a stream bank as part of the revegetation effort in the Klamath National Forest. (Photo courtesy of Bill McMillon)

lightning a chance to smoulder in the dry forests until they became flaming infernos racing toward consolidation.

As the fires spread, the fire crews grew, but always too little, too late. By September the small towns in the valleys and canyons were experiencing their own version of a "nuclear winter" as an inversion layer held the smoke and ash from the fires in low-lying areas until mid-October.

Fire fighters often had to use flashlights to read maps at midday and local residents became accustomed to driving with their car lights on during daylight hours.

For more than 60 days the fires spread. Even the army of 10,000 fire fighters that eventually assembled in the area could do little to stop them.

Jim Walker says, "We never really contained the fires. We just won by holding on until the rains came."

And the battle was far from over when the last embers were doused. Any forest that has been burned takes many years to recover, and one that has been burned to its roots, as were large areas of the Klamath, take hundreds of years without help.

Suddenly the USFS needed to garner enough personnel and money for an adequate recovery effort in the Klamath and in the five other national forests in California that had been hit hard by the fires. The fear was that the forests *couldn't* recover.

Out of that fear came the plans for Operation Phoenix, a program coordinated by Region 5 of the USFS in San Francisco.

One of the most important aspects of the program is its heavy emphasis on recruiting volunteers, both groups and individuals, to do much of the labor-intensive, backbreaking work involved in reforestation efforts and restoration of watershed areas.

What had taken the fires less than two months to destroy will take the USFS and Operation Phoenix volunteers over five years to clean up, clear out, restore, and replant, even with the 800 to 1,000 volunteers per season that Jim Wright is prepared to accommodate. After that it is up to the forest.

Volunteers inspect a completed check dam that will help debris and ashes settle before reaching salmon spawning grounds in streams and rivers downstream in the Klamath National Forest.
(Photo courtesy of Bill McMillon)

The first priority of the USFS is to restore the watershed. As soon as possible after the fires, grass seeds were sown on the mountainsides. And plans were made to bring Civilian Conservation Corps crews from around California to begin watershed restoration.

"If we lose our soil then we lose our streams, our fish, our wildlife, everything," says Fred Kreuger, Operation Phoenix coordinator for the Klamath National Forest.

To help avert this catastrophe, volunteers will work on steep mountain slopes to stabilize the loose granitic soils of the area and build check dams along streams where runoff containing soil and debris can settle rather than rush toward the trout and salmon spawning grounds on larger streams and rivers downstream.

They will also plant willow cuttings that will quickly

mature into shrubs along stream banks, giving the shallow waters much-needed shade so that both plant and animal life can survive the hot summers of northern California.

Another high-priority item is replanting the 15,000 acres of 15- to 20-year-old plantations of trees the USFS had planted in clear-cut areas in the 1960s and 1970s. These will cost about $1,200 an acre to replant if volunteers don't come forward.

Operation Phoenix volunteers are helping with the reforestation of the charred mountains in the Klamath National Forest.
(Photo courtesy of Bill McMillon)

All this work is hard, dirty, and done on dangerous terrain. Volunteers need to be physically fit and willing to do what amounts to slave labor.

"We're aware that many people won't volunteer for this type of work," Ruben Contreras, who is responsible for matching volunteers and jobs for Operation Phoenix, says, "but we want to be out front with everyone about the difficulties."

People who aren't interested in helping restore the forest may be interested in working on the restoration of 150 miles of well- maintained forest service trails that were destroyed by the fire. Almost 50 miles of those trails were part of the Pacific Crest Trail. A national scenic trail similar to the Appalachian Trail, the Pacific Crest Trail goes between the Mexican and Canadian borders.

Contreras had supervised the construction, along one of these forest trails, of three log, packstock bridges in 1986, and he saw all three fall under the onslaught of the flames of 1987.

"I would like to see volunteers who can help us with the reconstruction of those bridges," he says.

Other volunteers will work on activities outside the burn areas, replacing USFS employees who have been diverted to the recovery effort.

"I want to be able to find something for everyone who wants to volunteer," says Kreuger. "I want seniors and teens, individuals, groups, and families all to be able to have this experience."

He continues, "While the fires were a disaster, I think some excellent opportunities can come from them. Operation Phoenix gives the USFS a tremendous opportunity to reach out to the general public and to environmental groups, and it gives them an opportunity to participate with the USFS in the operation of their national forests. Maybe we can mend some of the old rifts with the environmental groups and give them a chance to have more input into the operation of the USFS.

Rothberg School for Overseas Students

Hebrew University of Jerusalem
11 E. 69th St.
New York NY 10021
tel. (212) 472-2288

Project Location: Israel.
Project Type: Archaeological digs.
Project Costs: Approximately $600 plus transportation to Israel.
Project Dates: Summer classes during July and August.
How To Apply: Send to the above address for summer school registration information.
Work Done by Volunteers: Normal archaeological dig work conducted during the hottest time of summer.
Special Skills or Requirements: The projects offered in this program are field schools that are part of the regular summer classes, and all participants must register as summer school students.
Commentary: Students from several hundred American and European universities are represented in this program each year.

Samaritans

5666 La Jolla Blvd.
La Jolla CA 92037
tel. (619) 456-2216

Project Locations: The U.S.; Baja, California; Jalisco, Guadalajara; Rome; Nairobi; Guatemala; and Mindeanao, Philippines.

Project Types: Workcamps, medical ministries, and evangelism ministries.

Project Costs: Vary, but generally between $200 and $500, plus transportation.

Project Dates: Mostly summer for one or two weeks.

How To Apply: Write to Darold Jones, Samaritans, at the above address for more information and application.

Work Done by Volunteers: Most projects involve building churches and chapels, with evangelism a second major activity.

Special Skills or Requirements: Volunteers must be strong Christians who are interested in evangelizing in the Third World.

Commentary: The Samaritans ministry has been completely reorganized recently, and they may be expanding their volunteer programs.

Saskatchewan Archaeological Society Field School

#5-816 First Ave., North
Saskatoon, Saskatchewan S7K 1Y3, Canada
tel. (306) 664-4124

Project Location: Lake Diefenbaker near Birsay, Canada.
Project Type: Archaeological excavation.
Project Costs: Registration $20 per five-day session, and $25 to $40 per day for room and board.
Project Dates: Late June to mid-July for stays of one to two weeks.
How To Apply: Send to the above address for application form.
Work Done by Volunteers: General excavation work.
Special Skills or Requirements: None.
Commentary: This field school has operated since 1983 and has been at Lake Diefenbaker since 1986. Participants receive complete instruction in excavation techniques.

Service Archeologique
du Musee de la Chartreuse
191, rue Saint-Albin
Douai 59500, France
tel. 27 87 26 63, ext. 355

Project Locations: Douai and Vitry-en-Artois, France.
Project Type: Archaeological excavation.
Project Costs: Volunteers are responsible for all travel expenses, plus 50 francs for insurance and registration fees. Room and board are provided.
Project Dates: Both excavations are open from July 1 to September 15, and volunteers can stay as long as they choose. A minimum stay of two weeks is recommended to become well integrated into the team.
How To Apply: Send to Service Archeologique at the above address for more information and application forms.
Work Done by Volunteers: Normal archaeological excavation work.
Special Skills or Requirements: No special skills are required although experienced workers are welcome and will be assigned more complex tasks. Volunteers must be at least 16 years of age.
Commentary: These two excavations are of medieval urban and small town sites. The work is an attempt to gain a better understanding of everyday life in towns during the Middle Ages. The excavation at Vitry-en-Artois is also interested in finding the villa remains of the Frankish king, Sigebert, who was murdered there in 575, and to find out what a sixth-century royal villa was like.

Service Civil International/U.S.A.

c/o Innisfree
Route 2, Box 506
Crozet VA 22932
tel. (800) 823-1826

Project Locations: U.S., Europe, Asia, and Africa.
Project Type: Workcamps.
Project Costs: From $20 to $50, plus transportation to site.
Project Dates: During the summer for two to four weeks.
How To Apply: Write to the above address for further information.
Work Done by Volunteers: Varies by camp, but mostly physical labor.
Special Skills or Requirements: Campers in U.S. workcamps must be at least 16, and in others at least 18. There is no upper age limit.
Commentary: SCI provides a way for people of different countries to develop close friendships in the process of doing valuable community service. Through practical and enjoyable work, volunteers live the challenge of international cooperation on a personal level.

Servizio Volontariato Giovanile

8.10 Piazza Vantitelli
Caserta, Italy 81100
tel. 0823/322518

Project Location: Caserta Province.
Project Types: Archaeology, environmental protection, forest
fire fighting, and other civil-work projects.
Project Costs: None, other than transportation to Italy.
Project Dates: July to August for eight weeks.
How To Apply: Write to the above address for information and
application forms.
Work Done by Volunteers: Varies.
Special Skills or Requirements: Interest in working in a multi-
cultural environment.
Commentary: This organization only accepts five volunteers
from the U.S. each year.

Severn Valley Railway Company Limited

The Station
Bewdley, Worcestershire DY12 1BG, England
tel. Bewdley 403816

Project Locations: At six stations along the railway, which is located to the west of Birmingham in the heart of the birthplace of the Industrial Revolution.

Project Type: Operation of a steam railway.

Project Costs: Volunteers are responsible for all travel expenses, arrangements, and meals. Lodging in old railway coaches is available at a nominal cost.

Project Dates: Year-round.

How To Apply: Write to Membership Chairman at the above address for information on becoming a member of the railway and for volunteer information.

Work Done by Volunteers: Every aspect of operating a railway, from working as engineer to painting the loo.

Special Skills or Requirements: A strong interest in railways, and a desire to work under supervision.

From Expedition to Life Change

A Gonzaga University undergraduate changed his major from philosophy to pre-med, and is currently a doctor in Washington because of his summer as an Amigos de las Americas public health volunteer in Latin America. A Philadelphia woman dropped out of her career in management and went back to school to obtain a doctorate in archaeology after her Earthwatch expedition.

And like these two, Joan Lewis says that her experiences as a volunteer became the catalyst for a life change.

"I stepped into my own unconscious by going to the most primitive area of Australia," Lewis says. "I had been introduced to Aboriginal art and Australia by the movie *The Last Wave*, and had become totally wrapped up in it when a coworker gave me an Earthwatch brochure of a trip to Australia."

That expedition, which took place in the summer of 1981, was to bring dramatic changes in Lewis's life over the next five years. The trip was a combination archaeological dig and cave art exploration that gave Lewis an early glimpse of what was to come on three later expeditions to the same area.

"While I thoroughly enjoyed this first expedition," Lewis says, "it wasn't until I returned to North Queensland in the summer of 1983 that my life began to take on a different focus.

"I returned to Queensland in 1983 partially to relive the experiences I had in 1981, and I wasn't alone. One friend from that first summer returned with me, along with about one-third of the first group."

The focus of the expedition had changed during the intervening year and was now being led by amateur artist and explorer Percy Trezise, a retired airline pilot.

He had located several sites of ancient Aboriginal art that had never been documented by Europeans, and, along with Dick Roughsey, an Aboriginal artist, one-time chair of the Aboriginal Art Board, and recipient of the OBE, had begun to catalog the finds. They applied to Earthwatch for volunteer help when they realized the extent of their undertaking.

Lewis was in their first group of volunteers. And, although neither they nor Joan would have thought so at their initial meeting, these two were to become a focus of Lewis's new life, along with Aboriginal art and Australian lore.

"When I got off the plane, Dick and Percy laughed at this 'Hollywood' type with large sunglasses, long, flaming red hair, and tight pants," she says.

As a Los Angeles native and an executive in charge of print advertising for a large corporation, Lewis now recognizes how out of place she must have appeared to this crusty pair of Australians. Not that they weren't an odd pair themselves, one a flamboyant Aussie and the other a sophisticated Aboriginal.

Lewis soon discovered a real affinity for the two, however, and with their deep interest in preserving the artifacts of a disappearing tribe.

"Seeing the work of a prehistoric society, and walking on the same ground they did, brought about some deep changes in my philosophy of life," Lewis reports.

She found it difficult to maintain the same interests and concerns she had held in Los Angeles. She says she became more grounded, and aware of her natural being, as she spent time in the forest of Queensland.

After the summer of 1983, Lewis returned to Australia for two more expeditions led by Trezise and Roughsey, and during those years began to study Jungian psychology, along with Aboriginal art.

By the end of the 1985 trip Lewis had found what she calls "her sense of place in the world," and that place no longer included the high-pressure job she had held when she began her "incredible fascination with all things Australian."

She quit her job, began to do freelance advertising work, and concentrated on writing a book on the friendship between an Aboriginal and a white man, one that seems to epitomize the Australian idea of "mateship."

Lewis's introduction to Trezise and Roughsey had been an introduction to a new life. It meant new friends, new ideas, and a new direction.

Dick Roughsey died soon after Joan Lewis left Australia in 1985, but her new life will forever have him and Percy Trezise as part of it. These two, who had been close friends for 25 years, made room for her and helped her through many changes.

Now she is attempting to give them something back. Since the fall of 1985 she has been completing research on her book about the two and is now working on the manuscript. By telling the world of their most unusual friendship, she hopes that others will discover something of the thrill of living on the same ground as primitive people who drew cave paintings to pass on their view of the world.

Shaftesbury Society

Shaftesbury House
2a Amity Grove
London SW20 0LJ, England
tel. 01-946-6635

Project Location: Dovercourt, Essex.
Project Type: Holidays for the physically handicapped.
Project Costs: Volunteers are responsible for all travel expenses, but may apply for help with travel within the United Kingdom.
Project Dates: Two-week periods between April and October.
How To Apply: Send to Margery Bell, Holiday Department, at the above address, for more information and application.
Work Done by Volunteers: Helping physically handicapped persons, many elderly, enjoy a holiday by the sea. During their stay volunteers help guests by escorting them to shops, beaches, or on other outings; helping them with personal matters such as getting up, washing, dressing, eating, and going to bed; and doing other general activities such as dining room duty and laundry.
Special Skills or Requirements: Volunteers should be between 17 and 70, and physically fit and alert. This is hard work that is stressful at times, and any previous experience with the physically handicapped is a plus. The society also looks for any nursing or medical qualifications, plus the ability to drive a minibus.
Commentary: A demanding but rewarding two weeks. The society is a Christian social work agency, and asks that all volunteers feel comfortable with their Christian goals and principles.

Sierra Club Service Trips
730 Polk St.
San Francisco CA 94109
tel. (415) 776-2211

Project Locations: Throughout the U.S.

Project Types: Cleanup, trail maintenance, and wilderness restoration.

Project Costs: $175 to $250 for registration and insurance. Volunteers are responsible for all transportation.

Project Dates: Projects vary in length from 8 to 10 days, and run between March and September.

How To Apply: For service trips, write to Sierra Club Outings at the above address for more information and application form. The Sierra Club begins processing applications for trips on January 7 each year.

Work Done by Volunteers: Volunteers on service trips generally do manual labor while building and maintaining trails or cleaning up and revegetating wilderness areas.

Special Skills or Requirements: Volunteers must be in good physical condition and able to work and backpack at high altitudes.

Commentary: The Sierra Club has the largest service program of any of the outdoor and ecologically oriented organizations, and is able to charge somewhat less for their trips than some of the others because their trips are subsidized by corporations, public agencies, and individuals. While there have been very few work-related accidents on the trips, team leaders are trained in first aid and survival skills, and the Sierra Club tries to have a volunteer physician on every trip. These physicians volunteer their time in exchange for a waiver of the trip price, and are not required to work on the project, although many do. Physicians interested in joining a project should contact Dr. Bob Majors, 3010 Anderson Dr., Raleigh NC 27609.

Sample Projects: Following are some projects Sierra Club volunteers have worked on in recent years:

Coyote Gulch, Glen Canyon Recreation Area, Utah— volunteers helped backcountry rangers clean up 13 miles of trails in this isolated area of sandstone canyons with arches, alcoves, oases, and Indian ruins.

Cranberry Wilderness, Monogahela Forest, West Virginia— volunteers helped repair the most popular trail in this 35,550-acre wilderness area that is designated as a black bear sanctuary.

Sucia Island, San Juan Islands Service Trip, Washington— volunteers were taken to Sucia Island, accessible only by boat, where they did trail renovation and maintenance.

Denali Park Restoration Project, Alaska—volunteers worked within site of Mount McKinley attempting to eradicate evidence of past mining activities in the park. Project ended with a 25-mile cross-country hike back over the tundra.

Big Pine Creek Cleanup, Inyo Forest, Sierra Nevada—volunteers spent a week picking up trash, revegetating campsites, and restoring the natural beauty of the area.

Salmon River Work and Raft, Klamath Forest, California— volunteers, all of whom could swim and had previous rafting experience, built one steep trail down to Cascade Rapids and roughed out a trail to Last Chance/Freight Train, both Class 5 white water. These trails were the first into one of the most technically difficult rivers in the country.

Sioux Indian YMCA

PO Box 218
Dupree SD 57623
tel. (605) 365-5232

Project Locations: South Dakota Sioux reservation communities.

Project Types: Community involvement projects.

Project Costs: Volunteers are responsible for travel and personal expenses.

Project Dates: Various times during the year.

How To Apply: Write to Sioux Indian YMCA at the above address for information and application form.

Work Done by Volunteers: Community recreation, working in schools, leaders in summer camps, etc.

Special Skills or Requirements: Flexibility, creativity, independence, and a general interest in people.

Commentary: These projects are sponsored by the only YMCA operated by and serving primarily Native American people, and volunteers must realize that all projects entail a commitment of 24-hour days and 7-day weeks during projects. Also, because of the poverty/alcohol syndrome on the reservation, all volunteers are required to abstain from drinking and drugs during their stay. Persons of all religious faiths and commitments are accepted as volunteers, but they will be asked to respect and participate in the Christian religious life of the community.

Sample Projects: Headstart assistant, nutrition program worker, community developer, and camp leader.

Southern Steam Trust (Swanage Railway)

Station House
Swanage, Dorset BH19 1HB, England
tel. 01 538 2521

Project Location: Swanage.
Project Type: Railway restoration.
Project Dates: Year-round.
How To Apply: Write to the above address for further information and application.
Work Done by Volunteers: Everything connected with the restoration and operation of a railway line, from building maintenance to laying tracks.
Special Skills or Requirements: Any skill can be used, but particularly appreciated are applications from volunteers skilled in administration, engineering, and conservation.
Commentary: This railway was closed in 1972 over the opposition of many local residents, as well as railway buffs around the country. The Southern Steam Trust is attempting to preserve the services offered by the Swanage Railway, as well as the historical aspects of it.

Strathcona Archaeological Center

Volunteer Program
Strathcona Science Park
Edmonton, AL T6G 2P8, Canada
tel. (403) 427-9487, or May–September: (403) 422- 5809, or October–April: (403) 220-7629

Project Location: Strathcona Archaeological Center, Edmonton.
Project Type: Archaeological excavation.
Project Costs: Participants responsible for all food, travel, and lodging.
Project Dates: Volunteers must agree to work a minimum of four days or two consecutive weekends anytime between mid-May and mid-August.
How To Apply: Write to Volunteer Program, Strathcona Archaeological Center, Dept. of Archaeology, University of Calgary, Calgary, AL T2N 1N4, Canada
Work Done by Volunteers: Excavation of site, and washing and cataloging recovered artifacts.
Special Skills or Requirements: Participants must be physically capable of doing labor comparable to light garden work.
Commentary: This program was initiated in 1982 as part of a public education program designed to increase public awareness of archaeology, and to give adults an opportunity to participate in an excavation project.

Student Conservation Association, Inc.

PO Box 550
Charlestown NH 03603
tel. (603) 826- 4301

Project Locations: Throughout the U.S., including Alaska, and Hawaii, Puerto Rico, and the Virgin Islands.

Project Types: Conservation and natural resource management.

Project Costs: None. Volunteers receive funds for round- trip travel from home to project site, free housing, a food allowance, and a uniform allowance.

Project Dates: Positions are available year- round, with most lasting 12 weeks. Volunteers work 40 hours a week.

How To Apply: Send to the Student Conservation Association at the above address for application and more information.

Work Done by Volunteers: Volunteers work with federal, state, and private natural resource agencies—most with federal agencies—as seasonal staff. The work is varied, and volunteers can do anything from research and curatorial work in libraries, to range management, to computer work. All volunteers have the same responsibilities and duties as regular seasonal employees.

Special Skills or Requirements: Anyone 18 years of age or older who is out of high school may apply for the Resource Assistant Program. While most applicants are college students, you do not have to be a student to apply. High school students may apply for a high school work group or advanced work group where they function as part of a group assigned to special projects.

Commentary: The Student Conservation Association is large, and it fills hundreds of positions each year with the National Park Service and other cooperating agencies, such as the U.S. Forest Service, the Bureau of Land Management, and the U.S. Fish and Wildlife Service. Many people who began their natural resource careers as student volunteers with SCA are now employed by these agencies. Unlike many other organizations listed in this guide, particularly those involved with conservation and ecological work, SCA makes a special effort to extend its opportunities to volunteers with physical disabilities. SCA has a list of positions that applicants with physical disabilities can do.

Sample Projects: Some positions that have been available through SCA are:

Alabama Cooperative Wildlife Research Unit—volunteer assisted a graduate student in radio tracking eastern indigo snakes on a refuge in northern Florida. Volunteer was required to have completed a college major in biology, or be enrolled in such a program.

Grand Canyon National Park Desert View—volunteer worked at Tusayan Museum providing visitor information, etc., for 60 percent of time and working in the field on revegetation work, archaeological digs, etc., for the remaining time. Volunteer needed background in anthropology and archaeology.

Hotchkiss National Fish Hatchery, Colorado—volunteer did hard physical labor feeding fish, cleaning production units, loading fish in distribution trucks, and general maintenance while gaining field experience in a fisheries resource operation. Volunteer was required to have own transportation.

Great Smoky Mountains National Park—volunteer worked in European wild boar control, including hunting and trapping boars at high elevation, surveying population, and other related activities such as computerized information analysis. Volunteer needed own transportation and experience in hunting, hiking, camping, and computers.

Grand Canyon National Park—volunteer did darkroom photographic work, including development and printing of black and white film, filing of photographic material, and some photography. This was one of the positions for which volunteers with physical disabilities were urged to apply.

Sunseed Trust

\# 10 Timworth
Bury St. Edmunds
Suffolk IP31 1HY, England
tel. 0284 848863

Project Location: Spain.

Project Type: Research into methods and systems of land reclamation.

Project Costs: About $70 per week, plus travel costs.

Project Dates: Volunteers may participate for 1–12 weeks year-round.

How To Apply: Write to Sunseed Trust, PO Box 2000, Cambridge, Cambridgeshire CB5 8HG, England, and send $3 for information packet.

Work Done by Volunteers: Research in appropriate technology, applied plant biology, gardening, and tree planting.

Special Skills or Requirements: No special skills except the ability to make routine readings and measurements.

Commentary: The work done by volunteers is sometimes physical, but generally interesting. All work involves research in how barren land can be reclaimed and made productive.

Tahoe Rim Trail

PO Box 10156
South Lake Tahoe CA 95731
tel. (916) 577-0676

Project Location: Lake Tahoe, California.
Project Types: Wide variety of positions available—trail building, construction and maintenance, fund-raising, office work, writing, photography, and environmental review. Many positions are year-round, but can be filled by someone who lives outside the area.
Project Costs: Volunteers pay for all transportation and other expenses. On some of the trail-building crews, food is paid for by the committee.
Project Dates: Trail building projects are held from May 1 to October 15. Other volunteer opportunities are year-round.
How To Apply: Send to Tahoe Rim Trail at the above address for information and application form.
Work Done by Volunteers: Seven separate committees use volunteers, and they need everything from photographers and writers for publicity, to attorneys, to fund-raisers. Volunteers working on the trail itself do everything from surveying to hauling rocks.
Special Skills or Requirements: An interest in seeing the completion, in the next decade, of a 150-mile trail around one of the most scenic lakes in the country. Data entry volunteers are needed for developing a master data base.
Commentary: There is no single uninterrupted trail around Lake Tahoe, and the Tahoe Rim Trail Committee is attempting to rectify that by using volunteers to plan and build 150 miles of trails. This is a grass-roots effort that is being joined by larger organizations (one of the American Hiking Society projects has been to work on the trail), and they are well along the way toward their goal.

Introduction to Appalachia for Volunteers

While great emphasis is placed on the work done by volunteers in Third World countries in Latin America, Africa, and other regions, little is said about the need for social action assistance, and organizations that provide such, in our own country. One region that has a number of social action agencies that need more volunteers is Appalachia.

The following article is adapted from information provided by the Commission on Religion in Appalachia (CORA), a volunteer-centered organization devoted to improving the lives of those who live in the region.

Wherever one travels, the impressions that are left depend upon the combination of personal attitudes and external experiences. The same will be true when you go to Appalachia. Some who come are overwhelmed by the beauty: soft green mountains, abandoned cars littering the roadside, unpainted shanties and mobile homes dotting the countryside.

The Appalachian mountains form the spiny backbone of the eastern United States. This whole stretch, which the federal government calls "The Appalachian Region" runs from southern New York to northern Georgia and Alabama. It contains 397 counties in 13 states, parts of Alabama, Georgia, Kentucky, Maryland, Mississippi, New York, North Carolina, Ohio, Pennsylvania, South Carolina, Tennessee, Virginia, and all of West Virginia . . . Appalachia is not a simple place. There are rich and poor, big and little, new and old, and lots in between. But somehow, no matter how confusing it seems, it's tied together by the mountain chain and by the coal in its center, producing energy within it. Of course, there is more than coal in the region. There is gas, timber, oil, farms, steel mills, cheap labor, herbs, and greens—but coal is central.

Some visitors come with an appreciation of the abundance of natural resources: the coal, minerals, forest, and water that fill the region. Others will focus on the sad fact that this natural wealth has made many outside companies rich and powerful and many Appalachians poor and powerless.

Coal in Appalachia has provided Appalachians with a very undependable and dangerous source of income. As long as there is coal and demand, people work. But when either runs out, the sudden and almost complete unemployment in the area creates tremendous tension in community and family life. Because there is little other work to do, young people must choose either to work the mines or move out of Appalachia. Staying means education will profit them little and going means leaving family and place, which are so important. Staying also means dependency not only on the coal supply, but on the coal company.

As it is now, much of the acreage in Appalachia is owned by absentee landlords—the federal government and private companies that own the land but whose decision-making headquarters are outside Appalachia, outside the control of the local population. Without access to the wealth of their home, Appalachians also lack power, especially the power to tax for local needs such as schools and roads, and the power to make regulations that could control the damage done to their environment.

Appalachia is green mountains and abandoned cars, love of family, and clannishness—much like the patchwork quilts you'll see for sale outside small homes. It is an intricate design of many pieces that together make up a colorful whole.

Those who bring with them a respect for diversity and a willingness to be quiet and learn will be enriched by Appalachian culture and values. The more pessimistic, how-

Volunteers help clean up around a newly renovated home near Crossville, Tennessee, in southern Appalachia.
(Photo courtesy of Commission on Religion in Appalachia)

ever, will see the isolation and poverty that have been nurtured by the same culture and values.

This brief introduction to Appalachia is meant to help you understand some of the patchwork, but only you can contribute the belief that God has given all humans gifts to be shared. The Commission on Religion in Appalachia and many similar organizations want you to share your gifts of time and talents with Appalachians. But we also pray that you will be open to receive the gifts the Appalachians have to offer you. Some will be quite tangible, like the best green beans you've ever eaten—grown, cooked, and served by the woman whose home you are winterizing—others you will have to look for, like the value she places on friends and family as she spends hours sitting on the porch talking to them.

We also hope that you will learn to ask again and again, Why? Why is there garbage in the water? Because they don't own their land? Why don't they own their land?

Ask why. Pray for eyes that see beyond first impressions and hearts that are opened by God's love. Then you will be both enriched and enriching as you work in Appalachia.

This article was adapted from material provided by the Coalition for Appalachian Ministry.

Suspension bridges such as this are common in Appalachia, and are often the only way to reach a home. (Photo courtesy of CORA)

Talyllyn Railway Company

Wharf Station
Tywyn, Gwynedd LL36 9EY, Wales
tel. Tywyn 0654

Project Location: Central Wales along the coast.
Project Type: Running a narrow-gauge railway.
Project Costs: Volunteers are responsible for all transportation and living expenses. The railway will provide volunteers with a list of recommended places to stay nearby.
Project Dates: Year-round.
How To Apply: Write to the above address for more information and application form.
Work Done by Volunteers: All jobs necessary for running the railway, from running and repairing steam locomotives to working in the gift shop.
Special Skills or Requirements: None necessary. On-the-job training is given if needed.
Commentary: This was the world's first preserved railway. The Talyllyn Railway Preservation Society, also a first in the world, was formed in 1951 to rescue this fine example of Victorian engineering. Over 65,000 people travel on the line each year, and thousands of others help by volunteering work and money.

Tecnica

3254 Adeline St.
Berkeley CA 94703
tel. (415) 655-9755

Project Locations: Nicaragua and southern Africa.
Project Types: Wide range of technical assistance and development projects.
Project Costs: Vary, but volunteers are usually responsible for their travel expenses only.
Project Dates: Regular monthly departures throughout the year.
How To Apply: Write to the above address to request application. Please specify whether you are interested in Nicaragua or southern Africa.
Work Done by Volunteers: Volunteers work in their areas of expertise, which include computers, printing and publishing, skilled trades, health care, teaching, engineering, etc.
Special Skills or Requirements: Usually volunteers have work experience in their skill areas, and some knowledge of Spanish is required for Nicaragua.
Commentary: Tecnica has sent over 800 highly skilled volunteers to work in the above countries since 1983. Volunteers should be interested in peace and democracy, as they will be working with grass-roots organizations working for social justice, economic development, and an end to apartheid.

Third World Opportunities

1363 Somermont Dr.
El Cajon CA 92021
tel. (619) 449-9381

Project Location: Tijuana, Mexico.
Project Types: Awareness programs to make participants aware of the realities of poverty and hunger in the Third World.
Project Costs: $20 for one-day experiences; costs for other short-term projects determined by project needs.
Project Dates: Projects and awareness trips held throughout the year.
How To Apply: Send an inquiry to the above address.
Work Done by Volunteers: Most projects involve house building in Tijuana.
Special Skills or Requirements: Construction skills and knowledge of Spanish helpful, but not necessary.
Commentary: Most of the work projects are done in conjunction with other groups working in Tijuana.
Sample Projects: Esperanza and Habitat for Humanity are two house building programs that TWO is currently assisting.

Travelers Earth Repair Network

PO Box 1064
Tonasket WA 98855

Project Locations: Around the U.S. and world.
Project Types: Vary from reforestation to erosion control and forest preservation.
Project Costs: Volunteers pay own travel and living expenses.
Project Dates: Vary.
How To Apply: Write to the above address for TERN application form; there is a $50 registration fee.
Work Done by Volunteers: Hands-on reforestation, erosion control, and farming. Also education and training of others.
Special Skills or Requirements: Depends on project. Various skill levels are accepted according to project needs.
Commentary: TERN is a networking service that links travelers with various projects around the world.

Trout Unlimited, National Headquarters
501 Church St., NE
Vienna VA 22180
tel. (703) 281-1100

Contact the regional offices listed below for information
about volunteer opportunities, most of which involve stream
work and fish management.

New England Region
PO Box 910
White River Junction VT 05001
tel. (802) 649-2747

Northeast Region
41 Vine St.
Port Allegheny PA 16743
tel. (814) 642-2882

Southeast Region
13400 Hiwassee Rd.
Huntersville NC 28078
tel. (704) 875-1505

Midwest Region
310 Water St.
Eau Claire WI 54703
tel. (715) 835-4093

Rocky Mountain Region
3982 Rolfe Ct.
Wheat Ridge CO 80033
tel. (303) 422-1564

West Coast Region
12 San Gabriel Ct.
Fairfax CA 94930
tel. (415) 453-5370

Turicoop

Rua Pascoal de Melo 15-1-DTO
1100 Lisboa, Portugal
tel. 531804-539247; telex 13566 Turcop P

Project Locations: All over Portugal.
Project Types: Workcamps involved in construction projects.
Project Costs: 5,000 pescudos registration fee.
Project Dates: Camps are for two- and three- week periods during July and August.
How To Apply: Send to the above address for registration information.
Work Done by Volunteers: Heavy manual labor.
Special Skills or Requirements: No special skills are required. Most camps are for those 18 years or older, but a few camps will accept volunteers as young as 15.
Commentary: This is another of dozens of organizations around the world that organize workcamps to help the less fortunate.
Sample Projects: Painting a school, repairing local paths, and constructing a playground are typical projects.

Tyrrell Museum

Box 7500
Drumheller, AL T0J 0Y0, Canada

Project Location: Alberta Badlands, east of Calgary.
Project Type: Dinosaur dig.
Project Costs: Minimal.
Project Dates: Summer. Volunteers should commit to a minimum of two weeks.
How To Apply: Send to Volunteer Coordinator at above address.
Work Done by Volunteers: Normal paleontology dig jobs, most of which are hot and dusty. Workday is 6:00 A.M. to 2:00 P.M.
Special Skills or Requirements: No special skills other than a sincere interest in the subject, although paleontology students are given priority. Volunteers range in age from 18 to 55. Summers in Alberta can be hot, and volunteers should be able to withstand the rigors of working in the midday heat.
Commentary: Programs are run at various sites in the Dinosaur Provincial Park and are selected as the need arises. The University of British Columbia Center for Continuing Education offers a field study program in the fall when there is sufficient demand. Write to UBC Center for Continuing Education, Field Studies and Educational Travel Program, 5997 Iona Dr., Vancouver, BC V6T 2A4, Canada; call (604) 222-5207 for more information.

United Church Board for Homeland Ministries
Voluntary Services Program
700 Prospect Ave.
Cleveland OH 44115-1100
tel. (216) 736-2100

Project Locations: Throughout the U.S.
Project Types: Community, institutional, and camp services.
Project Costs: Costs are minimal in all of these projects. However, volunteers are responsible for all travel costs and occasionally for room and board.
Project Dates: Projects are available year- round, and vary in length of commitment from one to six weeks.
How To Apply: Send to Carl Bade, Voluntary Service Program, UCBHM at the above address for more information and application. Application deadline for summer positions is May 1.
Work Done by Volunteers: A wide variety of service jobs are done by volunteers, most involve working directly with disadvantaged groups or individuals.
Special Skills or Requirements: Most positions require volunteers to be at least 19 years of age, but there are some openings for 17- and 18-year-olds. There is no upper age limit.
Commentary: The UCC Statement of Faith includes the phrase ". . . to be servants in the service of the whole human family." This simple statement best expresses the philosophy of the volunteer services program of the United Church of Christ, and all volunteers are expected to believe in that philosophy even if they are not members of a UCC congregation.
Sample Projects: The following are examples of projects served by UCBHM:
Perryville, Arkansas—six volunteers did animal care, office work, automotive repair, visitor contact, and construction on the 1,225-acre ranch operated by Heifer Project International. Their length of stay was flexible, and room and board was provided.
Washington, DC—one volunteer worked with the

Churches' Committee for Voter Registration, handling correspondence, phone messages, and a monthly newsletter.

Canton, Ohio—two volunteers supervised youth in two group homes operated by Pathways.

New Braunfels, Texas—three young adult volunteers worked with children at Slumber Falls Camp. Room and board was provided on site.

Workcamps

International workcamps aren't where political prisoners are sent.

They are part of a 60-year-old tradition, helping to meet real human needs and promoting international understanding at the individual and community level.

How do workcamps do this? By placing 10 to 20 people from 4 or more countries together to work on needed projects in various nations, and letting the volunteers and local communities get to know each other by working together.

There are over 2,000 workcamps held in Eastern and Western Europe, North Africa, Canada, and the U.S. each year, and a variety of organizations sponsor the camps.

The Council on International Educational Exchange headlined one of their newsletters with "Build a Better World in 3 Weeks," and that is what workcamp volunteers do. A CIEE volunteer from Denmark who worked at a camp in the U.S. wrote, "If you want to see the world in a different way, to take a more realistic look at the society, choose a workcamp."

And the experiences of U.S. volunteers abroad support his statement. Diana Wheeler, a Dartmouth student who was a Volunteers for Peace volunteer in the Crimea (USSR), wrote, "It never ceased to astound and humble me how these people would unselfishly offer me the best they had. . . . I believe that if today's leaders had the freedom or desire to take a trip like mine the future safety of this world would be assured."

Maine volunteer Elizabeth McKee was more personal in response to her stay at a camp in Spain. "Many nights my newfound friends and I would sit in a park in the cool night air and sing songs. I learned some new songs in Spanish, but what they liked best was when I'd teach them songs in English. Those simple, but very moving, peace songs were their favorites. After a long day at work, these quiet times were most welcome and these songs brought the evening a reflective time to look at what we had accomplished during the day. Though we may have vehemently argued all morning about capitalism and true democracy versus socialism, these differences were put aside. These evenings gave me hope and a new faith in the world."

While there is time to take local excursions and to socialize with locals, volunteers put in full days on projects ranging from renovating an old building in Turkey, to organizing a playground in Denmark, to making trails wheelchair-accessible in Oregon.

The latter was sponsored by an organization headquartered in Eugene, Oregon called Mobility International U.S.A.,

Volunteers from Germany, France, Wales, the Netherlands, and the the U.S. participate in a Council on International Educational Exchange project on the Lower East Side of Manhattan, helping renovate housing for low-income families. (Photo courtesy of CIEE)

U.S. headquarters of Mobility International, which was founded in England in 1973 to help integrate people with physical handicaps into various travel, educational exchange, and volunteer programs. Today it helps the disabled join the workcamp movement by locating camps across the world where they can participate as fully functioning volunteers, and by sponsoring workcamps where the disabled are joined by the able-bodied to work on projects that will benefit the disabled.

These projects are true people-to-people programs, and workcamps have been called "short-term peace corps."

Not all of what is learned at workcamps is about other cultures. The Ellis Island Project that CIEE ran in the 1980s taught many Americans more about America than they had ever thought possible. The project brought several hundred volunteers together to work on the restoration project of Ellis Island, and to work on the Lower East Side of New York with recent immigrants to this country.

Mary Morgan, a volunteer from Iowa, wrote about her summer: "Although the work on Ellis was mostly manual labor, our group was able to learn about what the immigrants faced. In many cases the living conditions of today's immigrants closely parallel those of earlier immigrants. Working in the Bronx with the New York Association of New Americans provided a unique opportunity to see the trials today's immigrants face."

A German volunteer on the same project said, "The government, the policies, and the people are three different things, and I think here we concentrate on the people."

And that is what workcamps are all about—people.

People who attend workcamps are interested in expanding their world experiences. Traditionally they have been college students or recent graduates who want to develop a wider view of the world in which they must live and work for the rest of their lives, but more and more older people are joining the movement, and for the same reasons. Two such volunteers are Bob and Lois Riboli.

A couple in their late fifties who had never been "resort"

CIEE volunteers help restore a fifteenth-century hamlet in La Roche sur Grane, France. (Photo courtesy of CIEE)

travelers, the Ribolis learned about workcamps through a newspaper column on working vacations that listed Volunteers for Peace, an organization devoted to placing volunteers in workcamps, and sent for their catalog.

They wanted a camp where at least one of the languages spoken was English, since neither spoke enough of another language to feel comfortable, and they quickly narrowed their choices down to several camps in Switzerland, where Bob's parents had immigrated from earlier in the century. Their first choice was full, which was serendipitous, for their second choice was to bring many surprises to Bob and Lois.

Bob knew little of where his parents had lived in Switzerland, and it wasn't until they arrived in Europe and talked to some distant relatives that they had anything other than the most basic concept about the location of Bob's ancestral home.

But family was not the first concern for the Ribolis as they reached Switzerland and joined their fellow campers at Castle Brione, a retreat for socialists and pacifists built over the years with volunteer labor. There they met octogenarian

Gerrard Muller is still active in the expansion construction of Castle Brione even though he is in his eighties. (Photo courtesy of Bob Riboli)

Gerrard Muller, the founder of Castle Brione and workcamp director, as well as the other campers.

"We didn't know what to expect," Lois says. "We were by far the oldest campers other than Gerrard, and we didn't want to be excluded because we were older, or because we were Americans."

They were in the minority in both age and nationality (the other 23 campers came from 11 countries of Eastern and Western Europe), but neither mattered in the long run.

"We were checked out by the younger campers," Bob said. "They wanted to know where we fit in politically. One camper wanted to know if we were 'capitalist pigs' or not, while others wanted to know if we were different from most Americans our age, but all were very accepting of us by the end of the camp."

In fact, both Ribolis believe their campmates were enriched by their presence, just as they recognize the rewards they received from working and playing with the young people of East and West Germany, Poland, Belguim, Turkey, Greece, France, Spain, Italy, and Switzerland.

"It didn't take us long to find out that our experiences were very different from the other campers," Lois said. "We drew kitchen duty the first few days, and we quickly became aware that the young children of a single Polish mother had seldom had fresh fruit. And we later saw how much harder that mom's life was than those experienced by most of our friends and children."

To Lois, the most striking example of that was how the mom spent her free time going through the lost-and-found to find old wool sweaters. She then unwound them for wool to make winter clothes for her children.

The purpose of workcamps is to work on constructive projects, and while Bob and Lois enjoyed the four to six hours they spent working each day, they also had fun with the other campers after the work was finished.

"We would go into the village at twilight to listen to the town musicians play in the park. The atmosphere was captivating, and we found that interacting with the local residents was as much a reason for being there as the work."

But for Bob and Lois this interaction was much more important than for the other campers. They were in Bob's ancestral home.

"We didn't know it until we got to the camp, but we could see my father's birthplace from our balcony, and could almost see my mother's," said Bob.

"We went to learn more about others, and we ended up learning more about ourselves," Lois added.

This they did by visiting with distant relatives and longtime friends of the family during their off hours. They even had a family reunion at the old family homesite.

Bob Riboli has a basic belief that people who work together break down barriers more quickly than people who are in social situations, and this belief was strongly reinforced by his experience at Castle Brione.

"We would like to join another workcamp," Bob said, "and we are looking for the right one to come along, even though it can't possibly match our first one. After all, you can only discover your birthright once."

Bob and Lois Riboli pose with Gerrard Muller, Castle Brione founder, at a workcamp in Switzerland. (Photo courtesy of Bob Riboli)

University of Alaska, Anchorage

College of Continuing Education
3211 Providence Dr.
Anchorage AK 99508
tel. (907) 786-1344

Project Location: Confluence of Shaw Creek and Tanana rivers 20 miles north of Delta Junction, Alaska.

Project Type: Archaeological excavation.

Project Costs: Participants are responsible for transportation to Anchorage and $15 per day for food and miscellaneous expenses.

Project Dates: Generally in July and August for five or six weeks.

How To Apply: Write to David Yesher, Department of Anthropology, University of Alaska, 3211 Providence Dr., Anchorage AK 99508, for application. Applications must be sent by May 1.

Work Done by Volunteers: Excavation of 11,000-year-old site with mammoth bones and human artifacts.

Special Skills or Requirements: Must be 18 years old, have high school diploma, and be in good health. An introductory knowledge of archaeology is helpful, but not mandatory.

Commentary: Project subject to cancellation if field school doesn't have a minimum of 12 students registered.

University Research Expeditions Program

Desk M-03, University of California
Berkeley CA 94720
tel. (415) 642-6586

Project Locations: Worldwide.
Project Types: Scientific research expeditions.
Project Costs: Costs vary from $600 to $1,600, plus round-trip transportation to point of departure.
Project Dates: Most projects are held between June and September, but there are a few held in January through March. Most are for two to three weeks in length.
How To Apply: Send to UREP at the above address for current information and application.
Work Done by Volunteers: Volunteers work alongside project leader and staff collecting and cataloging information. Field work is often hard, tiring, and repetitive, but also rewarding and exciting.
Special Skills or Requirements: Previous fieldwork experience is not usually necessary, but some general skills and experiences are helpful in getting accepted into this program. Wilderness, photographic, drawing, and diving skills are often asked for by project leaders.
Commentary: UREP is unique because it sponsors projects led only by scientists who are employed by one of the branches of the University of California. In other words, it is actually part of the University of California system, and there is no comparable organization in any other university system in this country. Volunteers, however, are from all over the world.

Upper Mississippi Valley Archaeological Research Foundation

2216 W. 112th St.
Chicago IL 60643
tel. (312) 239-1208 or (312) 233-1711

Project Locations: Central Illinois.
Project Types: Archaeological salvage and field school.
Project Costs: Approximately $200 per week, which includes tuition costs.
Project Dates: From early May through early August.
How To Apply: Request an application from the above address.
Work Done by Volunteers: Archaeological fieldwork, including excavation.
Special Skills or Requirements: None. The field school teaches participants archaeological techniques. Special arrangements are made for participants who are already skilled archaeologists.
Commentary: Archaeological exploration at Orendorf Village, a Mississippian settlement in central Illinois from the twelfth century, began as a salvage project in 1972, and has since become the site of one of the longest ongoing projects of its kind in the U.S. In the past two decades hundreds of volunteers have made substantial contributions to the understanding of this early settlement.

U.S. Bureau of Land Management

1849 C St., NW, Room 3615
Washington DC 20240
tel. (202) 208-5261

Project Locations: Most BLM projects are in the western states of Alaska, Arizona, California, Colorado, Idaho, Montana, Nevada, New Mexico, Oregon, Utah, and Wyoming.

Project Types: Volunteers work in a number of areas such as wildlife management, recreation, range management, archaeology, administration, and engineering.

Project Costs: Occasionally volunteers are reimbursed for some expenses, but generally they are responsible for all travel, room, and board.

Project Dates: Volunteer opportunities are available year-round.

How To Apply: Write to Volunteer Coordinator at the above address for volunteer application.

Work Done by Volunteers: Work ranges from entering data on a computer to installing rainwater catchments for deer and desert bighorn sheep.

Special Skills or Requirements: Some projects require volunteers to have special skills, while others simply require that you have an interest in volunteering and the ability to follow directions.

Commentary: Volunteer applications may be obtained from the volunteer program coordinators of the various BLM state offices. If you are interested in serving in a specific region you can contact the BLM office there for a list of available positions. The various state offices are listed below.

Eastern States
350 S. Pickett St.
Alexandria VA 22304
tel. (703) 461-1400

283

Alaska
222 W. Seventh St., #13
Anchorage AK 99513-7599
tel. (907) 271-5076

Arizona
3707 N. Seventh St.
PO Box 16563
Phoenix AZ 85011
tel. (602) 241-5501

California
Federal Office Bldg., Room E-2841
2800 Cottage Way
Sacramento CA 95825-1889
tel. (916) 978-4743

Colorado
2850 Youngfield St.
Lakewood CO 80215
tel. (303) 236-1721

Idaho
3380 Americana Terrace
Boise ID 83706
tel. (208) 334-1401

Montana
222 N. 32nd St.
PO Box 36800
Billings MT 59107
tel. (406) 657-6461

Nevada
850 Harvard Way
PO Box 12000
Reno NV 89520
tel. (702) 328-6390

New Mexico
Joseph M. Montoya Federal Bldg.
South Federal Pl.
PO Box 1449
Santa Fe NM 87504-1449
tel. (505) 988-6030

Oregon
825 NE Multnomah St.
PO Box 2965
Portland OR 97208
tel. (503) 231-6251

Utah
324 South State St., Suite 301
Salt Lake City UT 84111-2303
tel. (801) 539-4010

Wyoming
2515 Warren Ave.
PO Box 1828
Cheyenne WY 82003
tel. (307) 772-2326

U.S. Fish and Wildlife Service

Washington DC 20240
tel. (202) 343-4131

The U.S. Fish and Wildlife Service uses many volunteers for a wide range of activities. Some of their regional offices have individual entries, but you can also contact the office of any region you are interested in for a current list of volunteer openings.

Northeast Region
One Gateway Center, Suite 700
Newton Corner MA 02158
tel. (617) 965-5100

Southeast Region
Richard B. Russell Federal Bldg.
75 Spring St., SW, Room 1200
Atlanta GA 30303
tel. (404) 331-3594

North Central Region
Federal Bldg.
Fort Snelling
Twin Cities MN 55111
tel. (612) 725-3519

Rocky Mountain Region
134 Union Blvd.
PO Box 25486
Denver Federal Center
Denver CO 80225
tel. (303) 236-7904

Southwest Region
500 Gold Ave., SW, Room 3018
Albuquerque NM 87102
tel. (505) 766-3940

Pacific Region
1002 NE Holladay St.
Portland OR 97232-4181
tel. (503) 231-6121

Alaska Region
1011 E. Tudor Rd.
Anchorage AK 99503
tel. (703) 786-3486

U.S. Fish and Wildlife Service—Alaska

1011 E. Tudor Rd.
Anchorage AK 99503
tel. (907) 786-3399

Project Locations: National wildlife refuges across Alaska.
Project Types: Wildlife surveys, bird-banding projects, general maintenance, visitor center interpreters, and other such activities.
Project Costs: Volunteers are responsible for transportation to and from Alaska. Once in Alaska, housing and subsistence will be provided.
Project Dates: Some positions are available year-round for varying lengths of stay.
How To Apply: Write to Volunteer Coordinator at the above address for a full listing of available positions and an application form.
Work Done by Volunteers: A wide variety of game management jobs are done by volunteers, and most require hard work in harsh conditions.
Special Skills or Requirements: Varies by project.
Commentary: The National Wildlife Refuges in Alaska place about 175 volunteers each year, and the competition for these positions is almost as great as for paid positions. To help gain a volunteer position, you should prepare as you would if you were applying for a full-time paid position.

U.S. Fish and Wildlife Service— Rocky Mountain Region

PO Box 25486
Denver Federal Center
Denver CO 80225
tel. (303) 236-8152

Project Locations: Colorado, Utah, Montana, North Dakota, South Dakota, Nebraska, and Kansas.

Project Types: All aspects of fish and wildlife management and support services.

Project Costs: Volunteers are generally responsible for transportation to and from project site and meals while there, although there is sometimes assistance available.

Project Dates: Year-round for varying lengths of stay.

How To Apply: Send to Volunteer Coordinator at the above address for the *Volunteer Opportunities* booklet.

Work Done by Volunteers: Volunteers work at ecological field stations, wildlife management centers, fisheries, and other fish and wildlife stations.

Special Skills or Requirements: Some positions have special skills requirements, but most just require a desire to work.

Commentary: This region covers some of the most scenic and ecologically interesting country in America, and volunteers often get to spend all of their time outdoors in this outdoor haven.

U.S. Forest Service
PO Box 96090
Washington DC 20005-4788
tel. (202) 447-3760

Some offices of the USFS are listed individually, but they all use volunteers extensively. If you are interested in a particular region, you can use the addresses listed below to contact that region's office directly.

Region 1—Northern
Federal Bldg.
PO Box 7669
Missoula MT 59807
tel. (406) 329-3316

Region 2—Rocky Mountain
11177 W. Eighth Ave.
PO Box 25127
Lakewood CO 80255
tel. (303) 236-9427

Region 3—Southwestern
Federal Bldg.
517 Gold Ave., SW
Albuquerque NM 87102
tel. (505) 476-3260

Region 4—Intermountain
Federal Office Bldg.
324 25th St.
Odgen UT 84401
tel. (801) 625-5669

Region 5—California
630 Sansome St.
San Francisco CA 94111
tel. (415) 556-4310

Region 6—Pacific Northwest
319 SW Pine St.
PO Box 3623
Portland OR 97208
tel. (503) 326-3625

Region 8—Southern
1720 Peachtree Rd., NW, Suite 800
Atlanta GA 30367
tel. (404) 347-4177

Region 9—Eastern
310 Wisconsin Ave.
Milwaukee WI 53203
tel. (414) 291-3612

Region 10—Alaska
Federal Office Bldg.
PO Box 21628
Juneau AK 99802-1628
tel. (907) 586-8752

Put in a Switchback and You Get a New Respect for Nature

by Jeff Rennicke

One night in 1977, Kay Beebe was paging through the latest issue of *Backpacker* when she came across a National Hiking and Ski Touring Association ad calling for volunteers to build trails in Wyoming's Shoshone National Forest. The next day she signed up, and America's trails have never been the same.

Despite the blisters and tired muscles, Beebe was touched by the satisfaction of seeing a trail appear behind her and watching lifelong friendships blossom among the crew members. When the American Hiking Society took over the program in 1978, she volunteered to head it. "Volunteer Vacations," one of the biggest success stories in the American outdoors, was born.

That first year just two crews totaling 30 people were sent out on projects. In 1989, 250 volunteers participated at 29 sites across the country, contributing more than 17,000 hours of labor. Members can be anyone over 16 years old, in good physical condition, and willing to combine the excitement of a vacation with a lot of hard work. Participants pay their own airfare and a $30 registration fee. In return, they get food and a chance to help America's parks and forests.

It sounds crazy, but it works. More than half the participants each year are alumni of the program, returning to relive some of the best times of their lives. "The people who do this are wonderfully crazy," Beebe says. "It is hard but

Kay Beebe in her work clothes on a trail maintenance project.
(Photo courtesy of Kay Beebe)

rewarding work. Once you've put in a waterbar or helped reconstruct a switchback, you get a new respect for nature and you are doing something to help yourself and others."

Were it not for Beebe's volunteers, a lot of the trail work would never get done. With budget cuts in the Forest Service and Park Service, trails sometimes do not receive the attention they deserve. Montana's Flathead National Forest is a case in point. With 176 miles of trail, the forest has just two seasonal people on trail crew. The work load is mammoth. Volunteer Vacations came in last year with a group of more than a dozen workers and put in 56 waterbars in five days.

For her work, Beebe has received awards from the American Hiking Society, Gulf Oil, and others. But just as satisfying have been the letters she receives. "Thanks for coordinating the most memorable vacation I've ever had," one 67-year-old participant wrote. Those are the awards that mean the most to Beebe—that, and walking a stretch of trail completed by a crew from Volunteer Vacations.

U.S. Forest Service
Elden Pueblo Project
2323 E. Greenlaw Lane
Flagstaff AZ 86004
tel. (602) 527-7410

Project Location: Coconino National Forest in northern Arizona.

Project Types: Archaeological site excavation and documentation.

Project Costs: Participants pay $125 per week tuition, and are responsible for travel, and room and board at site.

Project Dates: Vary, but are usually for two to four weeks between June 1 and August 15.

How To Apply: Send to the above address for an application form.

Work Done by Volunteers: Excavating an archaeological site, restoring pueblo walls, screening for artifacts, and washing and cataloging artifacts, all under the supervision of professional archaeologists.

Special Skills or Requirements: No special skills, but a minimum of one week of work is required. Almost all work is done outdoors in dusty conditions with occasional rain, so a sense of humor is appreciated.

Commentary: An unimproved area in the national forest next to the pueblo is available for those who wish to camp. Potable water and chemical toilets are provided, but no electricity.

Talks on local prehistory and archaeological techniques are given throughout the summer, and there are numerous other archaeological sites and museums in the area.

U.S. Forest Service
Region 1—Northern

Federal Bldg.
PO Box 7669
Missoula MT 59807
tel. (406) 329-3194

Project Locations: All of Montana, northern Idaho, and parts of the western Dakotas.

Project Types: A wide variety of jobs such as campground hosts, wilderness aides, office workers, trail workers, and other USFS activities.

Project Costs: Volunteers are usually responsible for all transportation and living expenses, but some units offer assistance.

Project Dates: Year-round for varying amounts of time according to the needs of the USFS and volunteers.

How To Apply: Send to Human Resources Programs at the above address for further information and application.

Work Done by Volunteers: Backcountry cleanup, forestry technician, trail maintenance, wilderness ranger, and any other ongoing activities in the region.

Special Skills or Requirements: Varies by project. Some require special skills, while others only require a desire to work.

Commentary: The USFS is part of a cooperative volunteer effort called Touch America Project (TAP) that involves private sector sponsors—either individuals or groups—who provide funding or other support such as food, equipment, or transportation for youth between the ages of 14 and 17 who want to work on USFS projects. This is an excellent opportunity for youth groups to become involved with the USFS.

U.S. Forest Service
Region 4—Intermountain

Federal Office Bldg.
324 25th St.
Ogden UT 84401
tel. (801) 625-5669

Project Locations: All of Utah and Nevada, southern Idaho, and southwestern Wyoming.

Project Types: From fire lookout to backcountry ranger to archaeology technician.

Project Costs: Volunteers generally are only responsible for transportation to and from project site and meals while there. Some projects are able to give some subsistence pay on- site.

Project Dates: Some are available year-round for varying lengths of stay.

How To Apply: Write to Volunteer Coordinator at the above address for a volunteer opportunity booklet and an application form.

Work Done by Volunteers: Same as paid employees over a wide range of positions.

Special Skills or Requirements: Some positions require special skills, which are listed in the booklet, while others just require a desire to work.

Commentary: During 1987 the Intermountain Region and the Intermountain Research station had over 17,000 volunteers whose work was appraised at $3.9 million.

U.S. Forest Service
Region 5—California
Operation Phoenix

630 Sansome St.
San Francisco CA 94111
tel. (800) 552-TREE

Project Locations: Seven national forests in the region, which covers all of California.

Project Types: Restoring forests after devastating fires.

Project Costs: Volunteers are responsible for getting to project sites and providing own clothing and bedding. Forest service provides tools, training, and room and board.

Project Dates: Mostly from early spring to late fall.

How To Apply: Write or call the above for more specific information.

Work Done by Volunteers: Hard manual labor.

Special Skills or Requirements: Physical stamina, the ability to follow directions, and an interest in the outdoors.

Commentary: This project was conceived as a way of getting the national forests of California restored after the disastrous fire season of 1987, and it will continue for another three to five years.

U.S. Forest Service
Sequoia National Forest
900 W. Grand Ave.
Porterville CA 93257-2035
tel. (209) 784-1500

Project Location: National forest in the central Sierra Nevada.
Project Types: Campground host, ski patrol, trail maintenance, and general camp maintenance.
Project Costs: Volunteers generally are responsible for their own travel and living expenses, but USFS pays expenses under certain conditions.
Project Dates: Year-round, for varying periods of time.
How To Apply: Write to Volunteer Coordinator at the above address for a list of volunteer opportunities and an application form.
Work Done by Volunteers: Campground host duties, general maintenance duties, trail maintenance, visitor information, and ski patrol.
Special Skills or Requirements: An interest in outdoor activities and the ability to relate to people. Ski patrol requires skiing skills.
Commentary: Forest service projects often depend upon volunteer efforts, and without them many projects wouldn't even be considered.

U.S. Forest Service
Tongass National Forest—Petersburg Area
PO Box 309
Petersburg AK 99833
tel. (907) 772-3841

Project Locations: Petersburg and Wrangell, Alaska.
Project Types: Trail and cabin maintenance and campground host.
Project Costs: Transportation to and from Alaska.
Project Dates: Late May through August.
How To Apply: Write to the above address for a volunteer application form.
Work Done by Volunteers: Building and maintaining trails, maintaining cabins, and light campground maintenance.
Special Skills or Requirements: No special skills required.
Commentary: Located in southeastern Alaska, the Tongass National Forest is a rain forest with 110 inches of rain annually, and the region is surrounded by mountains and ocean. Access to most of the area is by plane or boat. Volunteers are housed in government housing; if board is not provided, volunteers are reimbursed up to $15 a day for food.

U.S. Forest Service
Tongass National Forest—Ketchikan Area

Federal Bldg.
Ketchikan AK 99901
tel. (907) 225-3101

Project Locations: Revillagigedo Island, Prince of Wales Island, Misty Fiords National Monument.
Project Types: Trail and cabin maintenance.
Project Costs: Partial cost of travel to Alaska.
Project Dates: May through September.
How To Apply: Apply to Volunteer Coordinator at the above address.
Work Done by Volunteers: Clearing and slashing brush, repairing boardwalks, constructing waterbars, installing trail markers and signs, cutting firewood, painting, cleaning, and constructing decks and other structures, and replacing stoves in cabins.
Special Skills or Requirements: This is hard, physical outdoor labor, and volunteers must be physically fit. Experience using hand tools is a plus, and volunteers must be willing to work in rough terrain in rainy, chilly climates. The cabins and trails are all in remote areas.

Retiree Is Volunteer Junkie

Since the first edition of this book was published I have often been asked about senior citizens, and whether they can join the projects in the book, as though they might somehow be excluded from the exciting challenge of volunteer vacations. While I often have tried to answer the question in general terms, there is no way I can give a better answer than the following article.

Volunteering and Travel Mix Well

by Betty Bicknell

Do you think because your family is raised or you are retired that your life is over? Wrong! You can be a volunteer. Find places where you can help locally, or do what I am doing.

At 61 I became a widow and at 62 my job ended. What to do with my life? How to use my time? Fortunately, a full-time volunteer for the Board of Homeland Ministries came into my life. She asked me to come and live with her in Rutland, Massachusetts, and work as a volunteer with the Heifer Project. I went and worked with them for three months.

Then I boarded Amtrak and went to Baltimore where I was met by a man holding a sign saying "New Windsor Service Center." Everyone was a total stranger but I found many friends. My job as a hostess and tour guide gave me an overall insight into the magnitude of the programs. This is where the Church World Service keeps many of its supplies such as blankets, layettes, school kits, health kits, medical supplies, and clothing. They also provide temporary housing for

Betty Bicknell helps others on the North Carolina senior program, operated by the United Church of Christ, one of the many groups she volunteers with. (Photo courtesy of Carl Bade)

refugees until sponsors are ready for them.

In September 1985 I received my next assignment through the Board of Homeland Ministries. I drove my car to St. Louis and proved that I could drive in heavy city traffic. Here I worked for a year in the office of a skilled nursing facility called Deaconess Manor.

September 1986 saw me on the road again, and I drove to Newton, North Carolina, where I work in a retirement village office. I am finding this so enjoyable that I have extended my time and will be here a total of two years.

Last winter I took two weeks off and went from the retirement community to Americus, Georgia to work for Habitat for Humanity. I may return there for a longer stay.

By giving my services to others, I have discovered that the returns outweigh what I have given. Another plus is that I've made many new friends who enrich my life. I also get a chance to sightsee in-depth because I stay long enough to get a greater appreciation of each area.

I like this style of living so much that I have sold my home and am free of all encumbrances. I hope to work as a volunteer for 10 years.

Some volunteers do maintain their homes and volunteer for a certain amount of time each year. Others, who are not able to be away, volunteer in their own communities.

If you do travel, in most cases your room and board are provided, along with a small stipend.

Try it! You will feel better physically, have a great sense of well-being, and be part of God's purpose, helping to serve others.

This article was first published in a column entitled "The Way We Witness" from the United Church News, *a publication of the United Church of Christ.*

V.H.H.
Asenvej 35
9881 Bindslev, Denmark

Project Locations: Throughout Denmark.
Project Types: Working on organic farms and gardens.
Project Costs: No costs to participants while working in program.
Project Dates: Throughout the year.
How To Apply: Send 40 Danish kroner to the above address and you will receive addresses of farms participating in V.H.H. projects. You then arrange your own visits.
Work Done by Volunteers: Working in the fields, cooking in kitchen, or helping to repair buildings and machinery.
Special Skills or Requirements: Interest in organic farming and the environment.
Commentary: Participants are expected to work three to four hours per day in return for food and accommodations.

Voluntary Workcamps Association of Ghana

PO Box 1540
Accra, Ghana
tel. 63486

Project Locations: Throughout Ghana, with some camps in adjoining countries.
Project Type: Workcamps.
Project Costs: $100 registration, plus travel to country.
Project Dates: For two to three weeks between June and September.
How To Apply: Either contact one of the organizations in the U.S. or Canada such as Volunteers for Peace, Service Civil International, or Canadian Bureau of International Education, or write to the above address for membership information.
Work Done by Volunteers: A wide variety of public service projects.
Special Skills or Requirements: Should be 16 years old or older, and be fit enough to undertake heavy manual labor.
Commentary: Another of the many workcamp associations around the world, Voluntary Workcamps Association of Ghana was begun in 1956 by a group of 11 men and women who wanted to direct the energies of young people in their country.

Voluntary Workcamps Association of Nigeria

PO Box 2189
Lagos, Nigeria
tel. 862997

Project Locations: Different parts of Nigeria.
Project Types: Primarily community development projects.
Project Costs: There is a $100 placement fee.
Project Dates: Between June and January each year.
How To Apply: Request more information from National General Secretary at the above address.
Work Done by Volunteers: Manual labor for construction and agricultural projects.
Special Skills or Requirements: Volunteers must be able to live in simple, rough conditions, work 40 hours a week, and speak English.
Commentary: Volunteers must have smallpox, malaria, and cholera vaccinations prior to entering Nigeria.
Sample Projects: Construction of a multipurpose community center in the northern part of Bendel State, and construction of roads in the eastern part of Ondo State and the southern part of Oyo State.

Voluntary Workcamps Association of Sierra Leone

PO Box 1205
Freetown, Sierra Leone
tel. 26501, ext. 221

Project Locations: Rural areas of Sierra Leone.
Project Types: Community development projects.
Project Costs: U.S. $150 per project, plus transportation to and from site.
Project Dates: Two-week projects held between July and September.
How To Apply: Send to the above address for application forms, or inquire at one of the U.S. workcamp organizations such as Volunteers for Peace and Service Civil International.
Work Done by Volunteers: Clearing brush, digging trenches, transplanting seedlings, repairing health centers, and other community service projects.
Special Skills or Requirements: No special skills except for medical projects, where volunteers should either be medical students or practitioners.
Commentary: This is a nonprofit, nongovernmental organization that is promoting international contact, cultural exchange, and rural development.

Volunteer—The National Center

1111 N. 19th St., Suite 500
Arlington VA 22209
tel. (703) 276-0542

Commentary: Volunteer is the national clearinghouse for volunteer centers around the country. If you are interested in volunteering in a particular location and would like information concerning the closest volunteer center to it, you can contact the above address for information. Volunteer also has a list of books on volunteering that they have compiled for their member organizations. The list may be of interest to those interested in learning more about volunteerism in its many forms.

Volunteers for Israel

330 W. 42nd St., Suite 1318
New York NY 10036
tel. (212) 643-4848

Project Locations: Throughout Israel.

Project Type: Work in hospitals, kibbutzim, local communities, or on IDF bases.

Project Costs: Between $500 and $895.

Project Dates: Participants depart weekly year-round for three weeks.

How To Apply: Call the above phone number for application and information.

Work Done by Volunteers: Volunteer work may include general labor, maintenance and repair, patient care, kitchen duties, gardening, geriatric care, and other duties.

Special Skills or Requirements: Good character and good mental and physical health, as well as enthusiasm. Volunteers should be between 18 and 70 years of age.

Commentary: Over 13,000 volunteers from the U.S. and 9,000 from other countries have joined Volunteers for Israel since 1982. These volunteers have provided great service to Israel and have enjoyed Hebrew lessons, guided tours throughout the country, and the hospitality of Israeli families on the Sabbath and holidays.

Volunteers for Peace, Inc.
International Workcamps
Tiffany Rd.
Belmont VT 05730
tel. (802) 259-2759

Project Locations: 36 foreign countries and the U.S.
Project Type: Workcamps.
Project Costs: $65 registration fee, plus round-trip transportation to camp.
Project Dates: Most are held from June to September for two to three weeks.
How To Apply: Send to Volunteers for Peace, International Workcamps, at the above address for information and application. Volunteers are advised to register before May 21 to insure placement for the summer.
Work Done by Volunteers: A wide variety of community service projects.
Special Skills or Requirements: Must be 18 years of age or over. No foreign language is required, but a knowledge of the local customs of the area where the workcamp of your choice is located is helpful.
Commentary: VFP is an organization with one activity: finding funding and volunteers for workcamps around the world. They are not a travel agency and do not book flights or tours of any kind. They have what is probably the largest selection of workcamps of any of the organizations in this guide.

Building Trails

Mount Shasta, a dormant volcano in far northern California, has drawn hikers and climbers to its slopes for years. The trail to the top has not been an easy one, however, and hikers have had to fight their way over boulders, snow, and glaciers to reach the summit.

Plans are under way to build a new trail that will make the upper reaches of the dormant volcano accessible to more nature lovers. While it won't take hikers to the top of the 14,162-foot peak, it will offer a leisurely 40-mile circle around the lower slopes of the mountain.

This isn't a new idea (the first recorded hike around the mountain took place in 1928, and people quickly began to discuss building a trail on U.S Forest Service land), but the method is new.

With a projected cost of more than $1.5 million, it is a wonder that the trail is even being considered in times of tight budgetary constraints on all governmental agencies. And it wouldn't be if several other long trials hadn't been constructed in the past decade by volunteers.

U.S. Forest Service Ranger Garry Oye estimates the trail will take from five to ten years to complete and will involve thousands of volunteers during that period. Over two-thirds of the cost will come from individuals and businesses, through donations of money and time.

Oye, a Forest Service recreation specialist, has several excellent examples of just how to use volunteers to build a trail. In fact, his 40-mile trail pales in comparison to the 15-year project headed by Gundy Gaskill of Colorado. Between 1973 and 1988 she was the moving force behind the planning

Volunteers use heavy hand tools to dig a section of the Colorado Trail. (Photo courtesy of Colorado Trail Club)

and construction of the 469-mile Colorado Trail, which extends from Denver to Durango through some of Colorado's most pristine wilderness. And while the trail officially opened in July 1988, Gaskill's work is far from finished. Portions of the trail still have to be rerouted, and all of it must be maintained.

Oye will pattern the Mount Shasta program after Vickie Raucci's efforts. She undertook the job of overseeing the planning and construction of the Tahoe Rim Trail.

The thought of building a 150-mile trail through two states, six counties, and three national forests during a five-year period brings to mind a large number of bureaucrats struggling for power as a multitude of governmental agencies fight over control and budgets.

That's the way it usually goes, but it didn't for the Tahoe Rim Trail, and all because of one bureaucrat, Glen Hampton of the U.S. Forest Service. He saw a need for a rim trail when he transferred to the Tahoe area in 1980, and he believed in volunteers and in Vickie Raucci, a dedicated director of volunteers. Hampton knew there were no public funds available for building such a trail, but he also knew there was an untapped resource—volunteers. Not only those who would volunteer money—from which more than half a million dollars will be raised by the time the trail is completed—but those who could give their time and energy.

Hampton wasn't wrong. He put in hundreds of hours of Forest Service time getting the trail started, and hundreds of others put in an estimated 10,000 volunteer hours before any construction was done on the trail. He also recommended that the Tahoe Rim Trail Committee hire Vickie Raucci as project director.

Almost 50 miles of the trail existed as part of the Pacific Crest Trail when the Tahoe Rim Trail Committee began work, which left 100 miles of trail to be built, as well as a number of trailheads where hikers could have easy access to the trail.

With an estimated 400 volunteer hours required for each mile of trail, Raucci, the only full-time paid Rim Trail staff

Volunteers put a retaining wall in place on the Tahoe Rim Trail, which is nearing completion. (Photo courtesy of Tahoe Rim Trail Committee)

member, had her work cut out for her. Forty thousand volunteer hours needed to be recruited and scheduled, and good crew leaders had to be found to lead each work group.

With most crews working only on weekends, and only summer weekends available because of the heavy winter snowfall around Lake Tahoe, Raucci and members of various committees had to recruit many crews to complete the trail.

Two summers into the project, they had found enough volunteers to complete 25 miles of trail and several trailheads. This put them on schedule.

When the trail is completed it will have taken more than a decade for volunteers to build the first trail to completely encircle the highest, largest, and most beautiful alpine lake in North America. The trail will allow hikers to cross meadows where Basque sheepherders roamed with their flocks 100 years ago, explore large groves of aspens and magnificent stands of red fir and ponderosa pine, and skirt the largest bog in the Sierra Nevada—all the while staying within a short distance of Lake Tahoe.

For the adventurous, a hike the length of the trail will take a week and a half. For the less adventurous, there will be a number of trailheads that give access to short legs of the trail.

What started as a dream in a newspaper editorial in 1973, and only began in earnest in 1980 when Glen Hampton transferred to the Lake Tahoe region, became a reality because of volunteers. But even more volunteers are needed to complete the trail, and to maintain it after its completion.

The Tahoe Rim Trail staff has developed a program they present to service clubs and other groups that describes the work being done on the trail and what they need to complete the project. Most important right now are able-bodied volunteers who are willing to use a pick and shovel to get the trail built.

To listen to Raucci is to believe that the trail will be completed by volunteers, and that it will be maintained by volunteers after its completion.

When asked to name the most important thing she has gotten from working with so many volunteers she answered,

"The knowledge that people can band together for a common good. If we can do the Rim Trial with volunteers then we can solve other, even more important, environmental problems in society by banding together."

Volunteerism does work. Ask Gundy Gaskill, Vickie Raucci, or Garry Oye. Or take a trip to Colorado, Lake Tahoe, or Mount Shasta in the next decade. You will see it in action. Or better yet, give one of the three a call and become part of the volunteer trail builders of America.

Volunteers in Mission,
Presbyterian Church (U.S.A.)
100 Withersoon St.
Louisville KY 40202-1396
tel. (502) 580-1900

Project Locations: Throughout the U.S., with some opportunities overseas.

Project Type: Church-related organizations, social service, medical, and workcamp projects are all available.

Project Costs: Volunteers are responsible for all transportation, but room, board, and insurance are provided on all projects. Many pay a monthly stipend.

Project Dates: Projects are defined as short-term, summer service, workcamp, and overseas health service. Summer service projects and workcamps are during the summer for 2–12 weeks. Short-term positions can be for any time of year for varying periods of time. Overseas health service accepts physician specialists for brief terms that fit in with vacation plans.

How To Apply: Write to Volunteers in Mission at the above address for more information about specific programs and application forms.

Work Done by Volunteers: A wide variety of social service jobs.

Special Skills or Requirements: Summer service and workcamp projects are more interested in enthusiasm than special skills, but many of the positions do require special skills and education.

Commentary: VIM is an arm of the Presbyterian church, and, although it does not require that volunteers be a member of the church, it expects volunteers to show a strong commitment to the Christian concept of mission.

Sample Projects: The following are some of the short-term and summer service positions filled by volunteers in 1990:

Juneau, Alaska—southeast Alaska Volunteers in Mission (SEAVIMS) used 16 men and women between the ages of 19 and 35 to work in teams of two to four traveling throughout southeast Alaska to teach vacation Bible schools, counsel at rustic Christian camps, and find other self-motivated ways to minister to native villages, tourist towns, logging camps, and cannery camps.

Glenwood, Florida—Duvall Home for Retarded Children used six volunteers for a variety of jobs in the home.

San Francisco, California—Donaldina Cameron House used 16 women and men between 17 and 22 to serve as live-in day camp counselors with 50 other young volunteers and 300 children in a multiservice community center for Chinese Americans and immigrants.

Abiqui, New Mexico—Ghost Ranch, a Presbyterian family learning center, used 38 volunteers for work learning program. They helped serve ranch needs in areas such as kitchen and dining room servie, housekeeping, lifeguarding, and ranch and farm work.

Volunteers in Technical Assistance (VITA)

1815 N. Lynn St., Suite 200
Arlington VA 22209
tel. (703) 276-1800

Commentary: VITA is another unusual volunteer organization. It doesn't sponsor projects, it doesn't organize trips, and
it isn't active in any one area. Instead, it is a clearinghouse
that attempts to match volunteers that have some technical
expertise with people and organizations from the Third
World that have requested technical assistance with
problems they have encountered while attempting the complex process of developing their economy. Most of the help
given by the volunteers is done by mail, but there are frequently problems that require the volunteer to be on-site to
help solve them. VITA asks three questions of anyone who
wishes to volunteer: Do you have technical skills that would
be of use to others? Are you willing to share them? Why do
you wish to be a VITA volunteer? If you can answer these
questions in a positive manner, and are really interested in
sharing your expertise, call or write VITA.

Volunteers Overseas Cooperative Assistance

1800 Massachusetts Ave., NW
Washington DC 20036
tel. (202) 223-2072

Commentary: VOCA is an association that uses government and private funds to help send highly qualified men and women from U.S. business cooperatives of various kinds to developing countries to help fledgling cooperatives succeed. While these volunteers are hand-picked from a relatively small pool of experienced people, a new program instituted by VOCA gives more people an opportunity to volunteer their services. This is the Farmer-to-Farmer Program. This new program offers short-term technical and managerial assistance to farmers in developing countries. In its first year of operation as a pilot program more than 50 farmers served as volunteers. These volunteers served for a maximum of 12 weeks. For successful farmers who would like to share their expertise with struggling farmers in the Third World this is an excellent program.

Washington State Parks and Recreation Commission

7150 Cleanwater Lane
Olympia WA 98504-5711
tel. (206) 753-5759

Project Locations: Parks throughout the state.

Project Types: Wide variety of park work.

Project Costs: Volunteers are responsible for all travel and personal expenses, but campground fees are waived.

Project Dates: April 1 to September 30. Length of stay varies with project, but there is a three-week minimum stay for campground hosts.

How To Apply: Send request for application to Camille Johnson, Volunteer Program Coordinator, at the above address.

Work Done by Volunteers: Office assistant, trail building, park cleanup, interpretive hosts, campground hosts, and basic repair work.

Special Skills or Requirements: Vary by project.

Commentary: Washington state parks offer opportunities for volunteers of all ages and all walks of life. They welcome applications from families, singles, couples, groups, disabled individuals, employed, or unemployed. They offer one-time projects as well as long-term assignments.

Welsh Industrial and Maritime Museum

Bute St.
Cardiff CF1 6AN, Wales
tel. Cardiff (0222) 481919

Project Location: All jobs are at the museum.
Project Types: Conservation and restoration of small boats, road vehicles, railway vehicles, stationary engines, and industrial and maritime artifacts.
Project Costs: Generally only room and board.
Project Dates: Volunteers are accepted throughout the year.
How To Apply: Apply to Curator at the above address.
Work Done by Volunteers: All types of work as needed for above projects.
Special Skills or Requirements: Project work is normally tailored to suit the skills of the volunteers.
Commentary: The museum has few volunteers from overseas, but is more than willing to have more. Information on how to apply will be sent upon request.

Welshpool & Llanfair Light Railway

The Station
Llanfair, Caereini on Powys SY21 OSF, Wales
tel. 0938 810441

Project Location: Mid-Wales.
Project Type: Operation of narrow-gauge, steam railway.
Project Costs: No fees, free camping, and hostel available for about 5 pounds per week.
Project Dates: Year-round.
How To Apply: Write or phone in advance, or simply turn up and ask for the manager.
Work Done by Volunteers: The railway is run entirely by volunteers under a full-time manager. Unskilled work is always available, and training for skilled jobs—locomotive operation, signalling, crossing guards, etc.—can be arranged in advance.
Special Skills or Requirements: None.
Commentary: This line is eight miles long and was built at the turn of the century as a cheap branch line. It has been run as a museum line for the past 25 years, and has locomotives and coaches from around the world.

Wildland Journeys

3516 NE 155th St.
Seattle WA 98155
tel. (800) 345-4453

Project Locations: Peru and Nepal.

Project Types: Trail cleanup and restoration.

Project Costs: Airfare to project sites, plus $1,180 for Peru and $1,395 for Nepal.

Project Dates: The Peru project is generally held in August and Nepal in late October or early November.

How To Apply: Contact the above address or phone for reservation forms.

Work Done by Volunteers: Trail cleanup and maintenance on the Inca Trail in Peru and the Annapurna Trail in Nepal.

Special Skills or Requirements: None, but all volunteers are expected to be in good physical condition, and be able to work at high altitudes.

Commentary: These are new expeditions to help maintain trails that are hiked by as many as 6,000 people annually, but that have received little maintenance by local governments.

Maintaining Trails

Backpacking is fun, and it is growing in popularity every year. But what happens to wilderness areas and to back-country after thousands of hikers and campers pass through each season? Litter accumulates as careless campers neglect to do the most rudimentary housekeeping, or "outdoors-keeping," and trails deteriorate from heavy use and hard weather. Who cleans up these messes and repairs these trails?

The answer all too often is no one, but for over a quarter of a century, and much longer in some cases, such organizations as the Sierra Club, the American Hiking Society, the Appalachian Mountain Club, and the Appalachian Trail Council have been aware of the damage done to our national wilderness and have had the foresight to do something about it.

As budgetary restraints have affected the ability of local, state, and federal agencies to construct new trails, so have they affected these same agencies' ability to maintain those already built. The above-mentioned organizations, plus hundreds of local and regional ones around the country, have stepped in to fill this void. And they have done it with volunteers who spend some of their outdoor time each year cleaning up litter, repairing trails, and generally keeping the onslaught of civilization from destroying our remaining wilderness areas.

The Sierra Club began their service trips over 30 years ago as their way of helping with the problem of backcountry maintenance. These trips began and continue as alternatives to the more traditional Sierra Club Outings. Instead of just using and enjoying the backcountry, the participants on service outings alternate hard physical labor with periods of rest and relaxation. Other organizations do the same, all with the intent to protect, as well as use, our natural heritage.

The first four Sierra Club service trips, which were only cleanup projects, brought out more than 15 tons of refuse from the wilderness. The projects have since expanded to include trail maintenance and wilderness restoration as well as cleanup, and the Sierra Club now offers almost 100 service trips each year. Thousands of people, young and old, have enjoyed the fun of wilderness outings along with the satisfaction of helping to preserve and protect our backcountry.

Appalachian Mountain Club volunteers use hand tools to move logs to be used in a retaining wall along a trail near Mr. Graylock in Massachusetts. (Photo courtesy of AMC)

Volunteers join together to move a log in the White Mountains. (Photo courtesy of AMC)

For the past several years the club has even offered a family service outing at their Clair Tappan Lodge in the Sierra Nevada, some 150 miles east of San Francisco. There, whole families can come to set up camp in the lodge, and the adults and older children can alternate days working on the projects, while the younger children are taken care of at the lodge.

So many organizations contribute volunteer time that each year Tom Lennon of the U.S. Forest Service estimates that more than 40,000 volunteers work with the USFS alone, most working on trails.

The Klamath National Forest of Northern California has over 1,000 miles of usable trail, and Ranger Chuck Smith estimates that at least 10 percent of those would be lost each

327

year without regular maintenance. And with ever smaller budgets allocated to trail maintenance the importance of volunteers is evident.

While the larger organizations operate on a national basis, volunteers can be seen in action across the country where literally hundreds of local organizations help maintain public hiking trails, primarily on USFS lands. There are more than 50 trail clubs in New England alone—plus the large Appalachian Mountain Club—and many others are scattered across the country.

All of these clubs operate on a volunteer basis, and contribute greatly to the maintenance of trails each year.

Agencies such as the USFS have become aware of the expanding volunteer effort, and have begun to solicit volunteers on an individual basis. Although previously they have worked only with large groups organized by other organizations, they are now developing their own programs, which include volunteers as a regular part of the USFS maintenance and construction effort to make the national forest more accessible to everyone.

Wildlands Studies

3 Mosswood Circle
Cazadero CA 95421
tel. (707) 632-5665

Project Locations: Throughout North America, Asia, and the South Pacific.
Project Types: Environmental and wildlife field studies.
Project Costs: $385 to $1,900.
Project Dates: Throughout the year.
How To Apply: Write to the above address for application forms.
Work Done by Volunteers: Full participation in environmental and wildlife field studies.
Special Skills or Requirements: No special skills are required.
Commentary: Participants can earn college credit.

Wisconsin Department of Natural Resources

Bureau of Parks and Recreation
PO Box 7921
Madison WI 53707
tel. (608) 266-2152

Project Locations: In all state parks and forests.

Project Types: Campground hosts, volunteer naturalists, maintenance and clerical, and ski or horse trail patrol.

Project Costs: Minimal.

Project Dates: Throughout the year, and length of volunteer stay varies by park or forest.

How To Apply: You must apply to the superintendent of each park or forest. You can obtain a list of these by writing to the Department of Natural Resources, Bureau of Parks and Recreation at the above address.

Work Done by Volunteers: Varies with each assignment.

Special Skills or Requirements: Knowledge of parks, camping skills, and general outdoor education. First aid skills suggested.

Commentary: This park system uses volunteers year-round, with ski trail patrols in the winter.

Witness for Peace

PO Box 567
Durham NC 27702
tel. (919) 688-5049

Project Locations: Throughout Nicaragua, Guatemala, and other Central American nations.

Project Types: Work projects with peasants.

Project Costs: $1,200 to $1,600. Many delegates finance their trips through donations from friends and churches.

Project Dates: There are from two to six trips per month throughout the year.

How To Apply: Write to Witness for Peace at the above address for information and application form.

Work Done by Volunteers: Working with the native people.

Special Skills or Requirements: Emotional and physical strength to endure the hardships of living in an underdeveloped nation and the political awareness to want to help the people.

Commentary: Witness for Peace is a faith-based organization that is committed to a nonviolent approach to life and the political independence of all nations. All participants must be willing to adhere to these philosophies while participating in Central America. Witness for Peace hopes that all participants will return home to work toward changing U.S. policy in Nicaragua and Central America.

Sample Projects: Delegates travel by truck or bus to the countryside where they join local worship services, work with locals on building projects, harvesting crops, and other everyday activities. The projects vary by time of year.

WorldTeach
Harvard Institute for International Development
One Eliot St.
Cambridge MA 02138
tel. (617) 495- 5527; fax (617) 495-9120

Project Location: Shanghai, People's Republic of China
Project Type: Teaching English.
Project Costs: $3,350 for the summer.
Project Dates: Mid-June to mid-August.
How To Apply: Write to the above address for information and application.
Work Done by Volunteers: Volunteers teach English at a special English summer camp for high school students in Shanghai. They live and eat with students, and study Chinese.
Special Skills or Requirements: All college students and graduates who are native speakers of English are encouraged to apply. No teaching or language experience is required.
Commentary: This program promises intensive intercultural contact. Volunteer teachers spend almost all their time with Chinese students—in the classroom, in the dorm, in the dining hall, and on regular weekend outings. There are small classes of five to ten students. Volunteers receive a ten-day orientation with teacher and language training involved.

Wyoming Recreation Commission

122 W. 25th St.
Cheyenne WY 82002
tel. (307) 777-6314

Project Locations: Throughout Wyoming at state parks and historic sites.

Project Types: Campground hosts, trail workers, simple maintenance, visitor information services, and interpretive programming including living history.

Project Costs: Volunteers are responsible for all travel and living expenses, although there are free campsites, some with utilities.

Project Dates: Year-round, although most needs are from May to September.

How To Apply: Contact Sharon Bollinger, Wyoming Recreation Commission, at the above address, for application forms.

Work Done by Volunteers: See list under project types.

Special Skills or Requirements: Ability to work with the public, mechanical and craft skills, and interest in outdoors or history.

Commentary: Many volunteer positions in this park system are tailored to suit the particular needs and skills of the volunteers.

Yee Office—Klostermolle

Klostermollevej 48a
DK-8660, Skanderborg, Denmark
tel. (45) 5/782040

Project Locations: Throughout Europe.
Project Types: Environmental and agricultural.
Project Costs: Vary, but moderate.
Project Dates: May through October, with most camps during the summer months.
How To Apply: Send to the above address for application and camp information.
Work Done by Volunteers: Various environmental and agricultural duties.
Special Skills or Requirements: Most of these camps are for youth between the ages of 12 and 25, but some accept older participants.
Commentary: Yee exists through the efforts of more than 40 youth organizations concerned with nature and environmental studies from throughout Europe. Yee attempts to spread information and knowledge about the environment through workcamps and seminars.
Sample Projects:
Montesinho Nature Park, Northern Portugal—participants helped research the flora and fauna in the park.
Kessi Wilderness Forest, Finland—participants worked in forest and in the community, attempting to block logging plans for the region.

Zoetic Research

PO Box 2424
Friday Harbor WA 98250
tel. (206) 378-5767

Project Location: San Juan Islands in the Puget Sound.
Project Type: Whale research.
Project Costs: Between $550 and $600, plus transportation to site.
Project Dates: Between late June and August for one week.
How To Apply: Send to the above address for application.
Work Done by Volunteers: Identification photography and recording underwater sounds.
Special Skills or Requirements: None but seaworthiness and an interest in whale research.
Commentary: This program conducts research on the minke whale, which was the most hunted whale species in the world when the project began in 1980, with more than 10,000 whales slaughtered annually throughout the 1980s.

Part Two

CROSS-REFERENCED INDEXES

These cross-referenced indexes were developed with un-decided readers in mind, such as those who may know how much vacation time they want to spend on a volunteer effort but don't know just what they want to do, or those who may have very specific ideas about what they want to do but don't know what is available.

The indexes are divided by project cost, length, location, season, and project type, so that anyone can begin with the most important item and proceed from there to narrow the choices.

While some of the indexes were easy to define, others were more difficult. Just what should be included in project cost? Where does one put the ocean in project location, especially if one year the project is in the Caribbean and the next in the South Pacific? And what should the category be for a social-action project offered by a religious organization that includes an archaeological dig?

The definitions were made, however, and imperfect as they may be, they are a starting point for readers who need help in deciding what type of volunteer vacation is most appropriate for them.

There are 18 subdivisions in the Project Type Index, 13 in the Project Location Index, 5 in the Project Season Index, and 4 in the Project Cost and Project Length Indexes. While these are arbitrary subdivisions, they will give readers a starting point in their searches.

A word about the Project Cost Index—some of the organizations, such as Earthwatch, include many things in their costs, including some travel, room, board, and insurance expenses. Other, smaller, organizations don't include anything but registration costs. This makes it almost impossible to compare organizations, so estimates given in the cost index only include the amount volunteers must pay directly to the sponsoring organization. This, in effect, makes some of the organizations appear inordinately expensive, and others deceptively inexpensive.

Be wary and check on just what is included in the charges and what extras you will have to pay. A trip to India that requires you to pay $100 to the sponsoring organization won't be as cheap when you add in round-trip transportation and room and board while in India; on the other hand, a trip to the South Pacific with round-trip transportation and room and board included in the charge may end up much less expensive than it initially appeared.

Project Cost Index

When using the following index be aware that these are only estimates. The total cost of any trip varies with individuals and where they are traveling from. Transportation costs to and from the project site or departure point—where the project sponsors become responsible for transportation costs—are not included in any totals. The costs to volunteers at the project sites and any expenses that must be paid directly to the project sponsors are included. Personal expenses can vary widely, particularly on projects where volunteers are responsible for their own room and board.

Under $500

$500 to $999

Project Length Index
Under One Week

One to Two Weeks

Three to Four Weeks

Five to Six Weeks

Project Location Index

In this section organizations are sorted by where they have
the majority of their projects. When an organization has its
projects evenly spread throughout many regions, it is listed
as worldwide. Those that have projects in several locations
but are not worldwide are listed in all the regions where they
operate.

Africa

Europe

Great Britain

Worldwide

Project Season Index

Project and expedition directors, as well as vacationers, often have their favorite season. Sometimes this is because their project can only be completed during some natural cycle. Other times it is because of seasonal climatic factors. But often projects are scheduled to coincide with the season when the most volunteers are available—summer.

In the following index, organizations that offer projects or expeditions in more than one season but not year-round, or that offer the bulk of their projects in one or two seasons, will be listed several times. Those organizations that spread their projects fairly evenly throughout the year, however, are only listed in the year-round section.

Spring

Fall

Project Type Index

Many of the organizations listed in this guide are involved in a wide variety of activities, while others focus on only one. The following listing is an effort to give readers an idea of which organizations offer expeditions or projects in each area of interest. However, some organizations, such as Earthwatch, offer expeditions that aren't included in any of the types listed. Readers can determine which organizations are most likely to offer unusual projects by seeing how many of the following categories each organization is listed under. Those listed under several categories are more likely to have unusual offerings that don't fit well into any of the following categories.

Archaeology

Community Development

Environmental Protection

Environmental Research

Public Health

State and National Parks and Forests

Trail Building and Management

Workcamps

Additional Resources

Below is a list of agencies, books, and periodicals that are concerned with various types of unique vacations. Volunteer vacations, learning vacations, adventure vacations, or a combination of the three are covered by these resources, and all add different perspectives for people who want to learn more about this kind of travel. Some of the books are published outside the U.S. and are not likely to be available in local bookstores. Their publishers can be contacted through the addresses listed.

Agencies

American Institute of Archaeology
675 Commonwealth Ave.
Boston MA 02215
tel. (617) 353-9361; fax (617) 353-6550

The AIA does not sponsor volunteer projects, but it does publish an annual edition of *Archaeological Fieldwork Opportunities Bulletin*, which lists excavation opportunities for volunteers and field school students, as well as some paid positions throughout the world. There were almost 100 pages of listings in the 1990 edition. The bulletin also includes listings of institutions and organizations affiliated with AIA that also use volunteers. To order this publication, write to the above address for current price and membership information.

Archaeology Abroad
31-34 Gordon Square
London WC1H 0PY, England

Archaeology Abroad does not run excavations, but publishes an annual bulletin in March and a biannual newsletter in the spring and fall that are available through subscription. These bulletins list projects and give detailed information about their staffing needs.

Dorset County Museum
High West St.
Dorchester, Dorset DT1 1XA, England

Each spring, the Dorset Natural History Museum and Archaeological Society produces a list of excavations taking place in Dorset throughout the spring, summer, and fall months of the year. This list gives information on the directors of the digs and whether they are looking for volunteers. The listing can be obtained by writing to the museum at the above address. Volunteers on these excavations are responsible for all transportation to the site, and room and board while there.

National Volunteer Clearinghouse for the Homeless
1310 Emerson St., NW
Washington DC 20011
tel. (800) HELP-664

This organization has one purpose: to help match volunteers with local service providers who work with the homeless and need volunteer assistance. They maintain a list of providers, the services they offer, hours of operation, and volunteer needs, which is available by calling 1 (800) HELP-664.

Books and Directories

Adventure Holidays: Thousands of Holidays in Britain and in 100 Countries Worldwide. David Stevens, ed., Vacation Work Publications, 9 Park End St., Oxford 0X1 1HJ, England. (Some titles from Vacation Work Publications are distributed by Writer's Digest Books in the U.S. and Henry Fletcher Services, Ltd. in Canada.)

Adventure Travel Abroad. Pat Dickerman, Adventure Guides, Inc., 36 E. 57th St., New York NY 10019.

The Adventure Vacation Catalog. Specialty Travel Index, Simon & Schuster, Inc., Simon & Schuster Bldg., 1230 Avenue of the Americas, New York NY 10020.

Adventure Vacations: From Trekking in New Guinea to Swimming in Siberia. Richard Bangs, John Muir Publications, PO Box 613, Santa Fe NM 87504.

Directory of Long-Term Voluntary Organizations. Voluntary Service Publications, UNESCO, 1 rue Moillis, 75015 Paris, France.

Directory of Low-Cost Vacations With A Difference. J. Crawford, Pilot Books, 103 Cooper St., Babylon NY 11702.

Directory of Overseas Summer Jobs. David Woodworth, Vacation Work Publications, 9 Park End St., Oxford 0X1 1HJ, England.

Directory of Volunteer Opportunities. Ellen Shenk, ed., Volunteer Directory, Career Information Center, University of Waterloo, Waterloo, ON N2L 3G1 Canada.

The Directory of Work and Study in Developing Countries. David Leppard, Vacation Work Publications, 9 Park End St., Oxford 0X1 1HJ, England.

Environmental Vacations: Volunteer Projects to Save the Planet. Stephanie Ocko, John Muir Publications, PO Box 613, Santa Fe NM 87504.

Helping Hands: Volunteer Work In Education. Gayle Janowitz, University of Chicago Press, 5801 Ellis Ave., Chicago IL 60637.

Helping Out in the Outdoors. American Hiking Society, 1015 31st St., NW, Washington DC 20007.

The International Directory of Volunteer Work. David Woodworth, Vacation Work Publications, 9 Park End St., Oxford 0X1 1HJ, England.

International Directory of Youth Internships. Cynthia T. Morehouse, Learning Resources in International Studies, Suite 9A, 777 United Nations Plaza, New York NY 10017.

International Workcamps Directory. Volunteers for Peace, International Workcamps, Tiffany Road, Belmont VT 05730.

Invest Yourself: The Catalog of Volunteer Opportunities. Susan Angus, The Commission on Voluntary Service and Action, PO Box 117, New York NY 10009.

Kibbutz Volunteer. John Bedford, Vacation Work Publications, 9 Park End St., Oxford 0X1 1HJ, England.

Learning Traveler, Vols. 1 and 2. Gail Cohen, IIE, 809 United Nations Plaza, New York NY 10017.

Learning Vacations: A Guide to All Season Worldwide Educational Travel. George Eisenberg, Peterson's Guides, PO Box 2123, Princeton NJ 08543-2123.

New World of Travel. Arthur Frommer, Prentice Hall Press, One Gulf & Western Plaza, New York NY 10023.

The Response—Lay Volunteer Mission Opportunities. International Liaison, Inc., U.S. Catholic Coordinating Center for Lay Missioners, 1234 Massachusetts Ave., NW, Washington DC 20005.

Summer Options for Teenagers. Cindy Ware, Explorations, PO Box 254, Acton MA 01720.

Teenager's Guide to Study, Travel, and Adventure Abroad. Marjorie Adoff Cohen, IIE, 809 United Nations Plaza, New York NY 10017.

Travel and Learn: The New Guide to Educational Travel. Evelyn Kaye, Blue Penguin Publications, 147 Sylvan Avenue, Leonia NJ 07605.

Vacation Study Abroad. Edrice Howard, ed., IIE, 809 United Nations Plaza, New York NY 10017.

Volunteer. CIEE, 205 E. 42nd St., New York NY 10017.

Volunteer Work. Hilary Sewell, The Central Bureau, Seymour Mews House, Seymour Mews, London W1H 9PE, England.

Volunteering in Literacy Work: A Guide to National and International Opportunities. Coordinating Committee for International Voluntary Service, UNESCO, 1 rue Miollis, 75015 Paris, France.

What in the World Is Going On? Opportunities for Canadians to Work, Volunteer, or Study in Developing Countries. Ingrid Knutsen, CBIE, 85 Albert St., Suite 1400, Ottawa, ON K1P 6A4 Canada.

Work, Study, Travel Abroad: The Whole World Handbook. Marjorie Adoff Cohen, St. Martin's Press, 175 Fifth Ave., New York NY 10010.

Working Holidays. Hilary Sewell, The Central Bureau, Seymour Mews House, Seymour Mews, London W1H 9PE, England.

Periodicals

Archaeology, Archaeological Institute of America, 675 Commonwealth Ave., Boston MA 02215.

The Directory of Alternative Travel Resources, Diane Brause, One World Travel Network, 81868 Lost Valley Lane, Dexter OR 97431.

Great Expeditions, PO Box 8000-411, Abbortsford, BC V2S 6H1, Canada; PO Box 8000-411, Sumas WA 98295-8000.

Real Travel, 301 14th St., NW, Suite 410, Calgary, AL T2N 2A1 Canada.

Transitions Abroad, 18 Hulst Rd., PO Box 344, Amherst, MA 01004.

Volunteer Vacations Update, 2120 Green Hill Rd., Sebastopol CA 95472.